HAS IRELAND A FUTURE?

Has Ireland A Future?

PEADAR KIRBY

THE MERCIER PRESS
CORK and DUBLIN

The Mercier Press Limited
4 Bridge Street, Cork
24 Lower Abbey Street, Dublin 1.

British Library Cataloguing in Publication Data
Kirby, Peadar
    Has Ireland a future?
    1.   Ireland, 1970 –
    I.   Title
    941. 50824
    ISBN 0-85342-869-7

For
Ciarán and Sinéad,
Myles and Kate,
Niamh, Sarah and Robert,
Matthew and Cahal,
who will inherit the Ireland
we create

Printed by Litho Press Co., Midleton, Co. Cork.

Contents

Introduction

I returned to Ireland from Peru in December 1986, having worked as associate editor of a weekly bulletin in Lima for two years. Even before returning, I remember friends advising me in letters to stay where I was, that there was nothing awaiting me back home. When I did return, many similarly expressed their astonishment that I intended to remain in Ireland.

The prospect of staying in Latin America was certainly tempting. While one came in contact there with something more of the rawness of life, any of the slight inconveniences were more than compensated for by the rich humanity of the people, by their vigorous sense of life, their infectious hope, their abiding struggle. I know of no one who has gone to Latin America who has not been deeply invigorated by the place and its people; it remains a deep privilege to have lived and worked among them.

Returning to Ireland was, therefore, difficult. To do so amid our deepening economic and social crisis appeared to some foolhardy. But it was also motivated by a sense that here the challenges are greater than they are in Latin America, that here more remains to be done. I have always reacted against the large number of Western Europeans and North Americans one meets in Latin America who appear to be escaping from the challenges of their own societies by throwing in their lot with the struggles of Latin Americans. While their commitment is undoubtedly to be praised, it has always struck me that it is far easier to join the struggles of other peoples than to be similarly involved at home.

Looking at Ireland from the perspective of Latin America underlines for me the immense challenges facing us as a people. As I repeat again and again in the following pages, it is not so much our immediate economic and social problems,

the situation in Northern Ireland, the evidence of a conservative backlash, that is most disturbing. These are serious
problems, but far more serious is the apathy and sense of
hopelessness that so inhibit any creative response to them.
Compared to Latin Americans, we seem paralysed by our
present situation and unable to aspire to a different future.
There a process of popular struggle is well underway; we seem
at a complete standstill if not retreating backwards.

It is out of a sense that we urgently need to name the
malaise gripping us, that this book is written. It claims to be
nothing more than a personal reflection on Ireland today
written out of a sense of acute concern at the direction in
which our society is going. Because I believe that Latin
America holds some important lessons from which we have a
lot to learn, the book in various places refers to developments
in that region.

This reference to Latin America may seem strange to
readers. If that is so, then I submit that both our history as a
colonised people and our present situation as a relatively
under-developed economy makes us far more similar to regions
like Latin America than to Western Europe, North America,
Japan or South Korea, all countries to which we are more
commonly compared. Many Irish who work in Latin America
recognise our ability to identify far better with the local people
than can North Americans or other Europeans. Such cultural
identification I believe to be but one immediate sign of the
deeper similarities we share as societies. Having read the
following pages, I hope many readers will agree that there is
much we can learn from Latin America.

Apart from responses to particular issues, there is another
important way in which we can learn from Latin America and
which informs this book throughout. This is what has come to
be known as the 'option for the poor': it offers the situation of
the poor and marginalised as the basic criterion from which
society is to be judged and makes them the principal actors in
the struggle for a new society of justice.

From this standpoint, no matter what high growth rates,

healthy export surpluses or declining rates of inflation a society can show, if these are achieved at the expense of growing unemployment and deprivation, then they are inadequate. The pages that follow look at Ireland from a similar standpoint.

The book is divided into three sections. The first, entitled 'Ireland in Crisis', examines what I consider the three major areas of crisis facing us. The second, called 'Resources for Change' looks at a number of areas where the Latin American experience offers us valuable lessons. The final section poses the question 'Has Ireland a Future?' and highlights choices to be made.

The first section begins with an examination of the hidden trends underlying our current economic crisis. These, I argue, are making the rich richer at the expense of the poor while they are making Ireland a more marginalised country within the EEC. Chapter Two looks at Northern Ireland and reflects on the nature of violence there, using analysis of violence from Latin America to throw light on the problems of the North. The final chapter in this section highlights underlying problems of alienation in Irish society and focuses on important lessons to be learnt from such phenomena as the moving statues and the two referenda on issues related to sexual morality.

The four chapters of the second section examine education, the media, the political system and cultural colonialism in Ireland. Each chapter draws some lessons for Ireland from the experience of Latin America and suggests how we might implement these.

The final section addresses more directly the question posed by the title of this book: Has Ireland a future? The section's first chapter outlines ideas for alternative economic and social policies which hold out the prospect of a better future for all. The final chapter examines the potential for developing an alternative social and political movement to help realise this better future.

Readers may find some parts of the book, particularly chapters one and eight, somewhat dry in parts as they examine economic issues. Let them be assured that they are not typical of the whole as other parts are more descriptive and may be found more readable.

Parts of section two, particularly on the media and on the political system, may be faulted since they analyse the mainstream media and political life in Ireland but do not do the same for Latin America. The comments on Latin America in both chapters concentrate on the responses out of which an alternative media and new political movements are growing. Any analysis of the mainstream in Latin America would point up a situation with many similarities to the Irish situation. What these chapters seek to do, however, is not to compare like with like but rather to show the sort of grass-roots responses arising in Latin America from which we have a lot to learn.

This book is not the work of a specialist but of a concerned commentator on Irish life. What it loses through any lack of specialisation in the different areas covered, it hopefully gains from the range of issues on which it comments. Anyone who comes to it expecting well-elaborated solutions will be disappointed. Even if such could be elaborated, to offer them would be largely futile since a better future can only be built by mobilising the creativity and energies of different sectors of Irish society.

What I attempt, therefore, is to give a fresh perspective on familiar problems, to encourage new thinking and stimulate some hope for the future. Since returning from Peru, I have been asked almost weekly to address groups up and down the country, adult education, church groups, trade union groups, political groups. What strikes me about them all is their hunger for fresh perspectives, particularly on Ireland, their intuitive sense of the serious malaise that grips our society and their concern to work for radical change. This experience constantly keeps my hope alive of the potential that exists to build a more humane and just society in Ireland. I hope that this book communicates some of the same hope to its readers and that it may help to release, even in a tiny way, some of the creative energies Irish society so urgently requires.

CHAPTER I

Ireland in Crisis: Hidden Trends

As it prepares to enter the twenty-first century, Ireland presents many differing faces. On the one hand are the faces of the young new rich, sometimes called the 'yuppies', confidently looking forward to new wealth and opportunities in the technological Ireland they are helping create. On the other end of the social scale, however, are the new poor, those increasing numbers marginalised by unemployment and with little or no hope that the future holds any improvement in store for them.

Growing poverty, particularly linked to high levels of unemployment, has come to characterise Ireland in the late 1980s. While a lot of public attention has been focused on the hardship this is causing many individuals and families, rather less attention is given to understanding what causes it. Indeed, substituting for any thorough examination of its causes is the widely created impression that it is almost an accident of nature. Failing to understand the causes of this poverty, successive governments fail to take measures adequate to combat it, especially through programmes to generate new employment on the massive scale now urgently needed. Similarly, the limited public recognition of the growing gap between rich and poor, allows our government to avoid taking decisive action to redistribute wealth in favour of the worst off.

Economic and social policy is obviously a contentious and difficult area. But this is not an excuse for non-professionals making a contribution to the debate, particularly when the professionals appear to overlook fundamental aspects of the problem. In this regard, it is to be noted that what little debate takes place in Ireland on these matters often fails to take into account the underlying trends which are leading to ever greater poverty and inequality. Such trends need to be identified, if we are ever to move forward towards more equitable policies. In particular, the failure to find a successful model of economic development needs to be faced. Furthermore, the contribution of our national debt and of the EEC to the widening gap between rich and poor cannot be overlooked.

'The New Oppressed'

Associated with the growing prosperity of Irish life in the late 1960s and early 1970s was a new awareness of the extent of poverty. Dr Séamus Ó Cinnéide, a Maynooth lecturer who pioneered research into poverty, has written of the 'rediscovery of poverty' around 1971. In a paper he gave at the famous Kilkenny Conference on Poverty in that year, Dr Ó Cinnéide made the first real attempt to estimate the numbers of poor in Ireland. His estimate that at least 20% of the population were living below the poverty line quickly became a well-established figure, being taken up by the Labour Party, the Irish Congress of Trade Unions and the Catholic bishops.

Ten years later a new figure captured public attention when economist and Labour Party councillor, Eithne FitzGerald, published a study in which she concluded that in 1973 about 30% of households in Ireland could be regarded as poor. This figure, translated as *One Million Poor*, became the title of the book in which her study was published in 1981.[1]

Quantifying the number of poor had as its object the elimination of poverty and the ending of social injustice. Governments in the 1970s made this a priority of their social policies, largely through real increases in social welfare benefits and the introduction of new benefits for groups inadequately covered such as deserted wives, unmarried mothers and older single women below pensionable age. The results of this almost decade-long effort were examined in a major study by John D. Roche. This showed that by 1980 government policies had succeeded in almost halving the risk of poverty but that at least 12% of households still lived below the poverty line. The author himself admits, however, that his figure is likely to under-estimate the real extent of poverty. Raising the level he set for the poverty line, he allows that up to a quarter of households could be classified as poor.

Evaluating levels of poverty with any exactitude is very difficult; comparing the results of different researchers is hazardous. Underlying the differing statistics, however, is the reality of poverty as experienced by many urban and rural Irish people today. As one islandman from the west of Ireland put it at a conference in 1981 which brought together urban and rural poor to share their experiences: 'I'll admit that an unemployed man in El Salvador might suffer a thousand times more physically because he doesn't have the dole that cushions the unemployed here in Ireland. But a sensitive human being in this country, condemned to a life of unemployment, can suffer just as much psychologically, mentally and spiritually as any Salvadorean.'

This expresses the deeper reality of poverty in a way entirely missed by the statistics. More than absolute material deprivation, poverty is rooted in powerlessness, in the experience of being insignificant. Again and again at that particular conference, participants referred to the fact that they were either rejected or ignored by the more powerful in society be they civil servants, politicians, priests or doctors. Over recent years, many middle class people who have had to sign on for unemployment assistance have found the experience a jarring reminder of the demeaning way in which the social welfare system treats the poor.

Sometimes referred to as the 'poverty trap', this situation of powerlessness reminds us that poverty is relative. A member of an Amazon tribe with almost no material possessions or income cannot be called poor if they can participate actively in their society. On the other hand, someone in the United States with a house and a car can very properly be called poor if they are black and live in a ghetto.

Older Irish people who remember far more frugal living conditions than those experienced even by people on the dole today sometimes complain that there is no real poverty any more in Ireland. While Irish people in the past certainly faced lives of grim and unrelenting poverty, the level of marginalisation and powerlessness felt by many today, compared to the higher living standards and expectations of the wider society, constitutes a very real experience of poverty.

A more revealing measure of poverty in our society, therefore, is income distribution. In his 1980 study Roche found a degree of income inequality which he called 'extreme'. He found that the richest 10% of Irish society had 30% of direct income which was more than the lowest 60% had. This refers to the amount of income before the top 10% pay their taxes or before the bottom 60% receive any social welfare payments. Even after taxation and social welfare, however, he found that the top 10% receive 25% of the national income, more than the lowest 40% receive. Altogether the top 30% of Irish households receive 52% of income even after they have been taxed.[2]

On the other end of the scale the picture is equally disturbing. The bottom 30% receive only 4.2% of direct income, that is before they are paid social welfare benefits. After they have received these benefits, their actual disposable income goes up to 13.6%, still very low in comparison to the richest 30%. As Roche remarks: 'Although there may be no question of discontinuing these payments, it may be sobering for critics of the welfare state to realise how important they are in avoiding destitution. The result illustrates the failure of the social system, despite large advances in output and wealth, to reduce income dependency in the community.'[3]

Covering a period of far greater economic success in the Irish economy than has been the case in the 1980s, Roche's findings underline some very disturbing trends. Despite the strongly voiced pledge of the incoming coalition government in 1973 to make the elimination of poverty and social injustice 'a major priority' and to lay the foundations of 'long-term policy that will root out the causes of low incomes', Roche shows that the rich got slightly richer and the poor slightly poorer between 1973 and 1980 in terms of the amount of money they could actually earn for themselves. Only through the effects of taxation on the rich and social welfare benefits on the poor was the imbalance redressed slightly in favour of the poor so that the 30% of the poorest had slightly more spending money in 1980 compared to 1973 and the 30% of the richest slightly less.

While his study confirms the effect of taxation and social welfare payments in redistributing income from rich to poor (though only very slightly), what is most disturbing is that the real underlying trend was making the rich richer and the poor poorer. This trend is certain to have greatly accelerated in the 1980s with the impact of mass unemployment. The amount of people out of work in the late 1980s had almost trebled since 1980 thus dramatically decreasing the direct earning ability of the poorest. As a result it is estimated that more than 1.3 million Irish people are now dependent on social welfare, over a third of the population. Yet while more and more are forced to depend on the state for an income, the numbers of those employed and in a position to pay the taxes to support such a social welfare system have been steadily declining.

Equally important is the reality acknowledged by the Commission on Social Welfare in its report published in 1986. This recommended a minimum income of between £50 and £60 a week for a single person to meet their basic needs, almost double the level of unemployment assistance at the time. This draws dramatic attention to just how inadequate are present levels of social welfare payments and underlines that dependence on these payments is in no way a protection against poverty. As Roche concludes in his study: 'The danger in the years ahead is not that there will be no economic progress but that it will be insufficient to loosen the growing tensions in Irish society. The greatest source of that tension is unemployment. Unemployment is the biggest threat to public policy on combating poverty. It leads directly to an increase in poverty in the short term, while indirectly it threatens to undermine the whole edifice of the welfare state in the long run.'[4]

The years ahead, therefore, look extremely grim. Even the most optimistic economists and politicians hold out no prospect for any substantial decline in unemployment in the foreseeable future. Meanwhile our society is learning to accept as normal that some 20% of the labour force is unable to find any work and more and more of our young people opt to leave Ireland. We suddenly find ourselves back in the situation which characterised Irish society up to the late 1950s except that our situation is all the more depressing since the growth of the 1960s and 1970s had led us to believe that it was possible to provide a decent livelihood for all on this island.

Yet, the one hope is that it now may be more difficult to persuade us to accept such levels of poverty and unemployment as normal. As the National Conference of Priests of Ireland put it in a statement in 1983: 'Anything which denies the opportunity to work or devalues it diminishes human dignity. Unemployment, leading to inactivity and purposelessness, is an evil which can never be an option for the human person. The unemployed are the new oppressed in our society.'[5]

An Under-developed Economy

In one of the main conclusions he draws from his study, Roche focuses on the limitations of social policies to combat poverty and instead draws attention to the need for adequate economic policies: 'There is no surer way of increasing poverty or inequality than through unemployment. Unless the rise in unemployment is halted and reversed poverty will intensify and anti-poverty policy will become increasingly a holding operation. If there is an overall conclusion to be drawn from the study it is that, while income maintenance policy was quite successful in reducing financial poverty in the period under review, economic policy was singularly unsuccessful."[6]

The more fundamental factor underlying the growth of poverty and inequality in Ireland is the continuing failure of successive governments since independence to find a model of economic development that could offer a decent livelihood to the relatively small population of this state. To this extent Ireland mirrors the situation of most so-called Third World countries, where the majority of the population has been relegated to the margins of the economy, unable to find steady work or to share in the wealth generated. While the new job prospects of the 1960s and 1970s seemed to offer promise that a new era of full employment was at hand, the grim reality of economic decline in the 1980s underlines the fundamentally Third World nature of our economy.

The factor which most cloaks this fact is emigration. Unlike in other under-developed countries, emigration from Ireland has acted as a safety valve allowing us to keep the numbers unemployed at home at relatively low levels. For example, between 1926 and 1971 some one million emigrated from Ireland. If they had stayed at home, as would have been the case if Ireland was part of Latin America, Africa or Asia, then our plight today would look much more like that of the Third World. Not only would the majority of our workforce be unemployed but overall living standards would also be far lower. Emigration has therefore placed us in a privileged position among the under-developed countries of the world; while many Latin Americans aspire to emigrate to the United States, the opportunities for doing so, either legally or illegally, are far more restricted than they are for the average Irish person.

Looked at more closely, our economy is more similar to a Third World economy than to a First World one. We have a far larger proportion of our workforce in agriculture than do our neighbouring countries, we have industrialised only in recent decades and our native industrial base remains weak. Instead we rely on foreign multinational companies for much of our industrial exports. Finally, like many Third World countries, we have built up a crippling national debt.

Ireland's failure to find a sustainable model of economic development is most apparent in our reliance on multinational companies. This has been the linchpin of the country's industrial strategy since the 1960s. Competing with similar agencies in developed and under-developed countries around the world, the Industrial Development Authority (IDA) offered generous concessions to multinational companies, most of them from the United States, to set up here. Among these concessions were extremely low corporation tax, the freedom to expatriate profits and generous grants towards buildings and training of the labour force. Adding to these material incentives were other important considerations such as political stability, a well-educated workforce and the wholehearted backing given to this strategy by successive Ministers for Industry and Commerce. Hard-nosed multinational entrepreneurs were impressed at the lengths Ireland was willing to go to attract them in. By 1983, there were 800 foreign-owned firms in Ireland, employing 77,000 people or 34% of the country's manufacturing workforce.

The inroads of these multinational companies in the 1960s and 1970s was associated in the public mind with the growth of a new prosperity in Ireland. But the costs were many, as is recently becoming apparent. In the years 1981-86 alone, for example, the IDA spent over £1bn in grants to multinational companies yet in those years the numbers employed by the multinationals here actually fell by 10,000! Between 1973 and 1980 the IDA is estimated to have spent about double that figure, these being the years when most multinationals were attracted. Yet, net employment in that sector grew by a mere 21,379 in the 1970s. This is seen by economists as an indication that we can expect little new growth in employment from the multinational sector in the future. Investment by US multinationals peaked in the 1979-81 period and has been falling off since.

If the amount of money spent by the Irish state to attract and keep the multinationals has proved very expensive in relation to the amount of jobs it succeeded in creating, these foreign companies have also done little to promote growth in other sectors of the Irish economy. In recent years, the type of companies which came to Ireland have been largely producing technologically advanced products, such as chemicals, machinery and electronics. So many US computer firms set up here, that in the early 1980s Ireland was the world's largest exporter of digital computers after the United States. The firms set up in Ireland by these companies tend to involve only certain stages of production. This means that they mostly import the materials they use, rather than buying materials in Ireland and thus stimulating other sectors of the economy. IDA studies have shown that foreign companies only spend in Ireland 44% of what they earn from sales whereas Irish firms spend 79%. Finally, the multinationals, even though they contribute in a major way to Ireland's export performance, repatriate most of their profits back to their country of origin. It is estimated that in 1987 alone, £1.4bn left the country in the form of profits, royalties and dividends. Little wonder that the IDA promotes Ireland as 'the most profitable industrial location in Europe'. This explains why Ireland's very healthy export performance in recent years has not translated into jobs and economic growth back at home – most of the benefits have gone to the multinationals and little to the Irish economy.

The long-term failure of successive governments' economic strategy is seen clearly in the fact that employment fell from 236,370 in 1981 to 208,232 in 1986. While the state was spending huge sums of money in trying to foster industrial growth, employment was actually falling. It should now be obvious to all that a radically different strategy is needed if we hope to stimulate economic growth that can benefit the whole economy and create sustainable jobs on a large scale.

The National Debt

Adding to the failure of economic strategy has been the burden of our huge national debt. This also has served to make the rich richer at the expense of the poor. Ireland owes far more to foreign bankers than do the most heavily indebted Latin American countries. Every Irish person owed IR£2,768 to foreign bankers at the end of 1987 whereas the highest equivalent figure for Latin America is from Venezuela at IR£1,250. Every Argentinian owes IR£1,000, every Chilean IR£960, every Mexican IR£760 and every Brazilian a mere IR£500. On top of our IR£9.70bn foreign debt, the Irish government owes IR£16.65bn at home, the equivalent of IR£4,757 per person. Taken on a per capita basis, therefore, Ireland is by far the most indebted nation in the world, worse even than the United States where each person owes IR£5,965.

Though Irish governments have been borrowing money since the 1950s, they were doing so for capital investment to build up the economy. It was the impact of the international oil price rise in 1973 which led the then coalition government of Liam Cosgrave to resort to borrowing simply to cover its current budget deficit, or the shortfall between what it took in in taxes and the amount it spent. It was the Fianna Fáil government of 1977-81, however, which really began the dependence on foreign borrowing when it decided to fund various tax cuts and the abolition of rates by increased borrowing. From then on the debt burden increased rapidly. From being 58% of Gross National Product in 1972, it climbed to 80% by 1980 and to 151.6% by 1987.

Those who benefited most from this heavy borrowing were the middle class. It was they who gained from the abolition of rates in 1977 and the other tax cuts then introduced. It is important to note also that while some taxes abolished in 1977, such as car tax, were later re-introduced, no property tax has yet replaced the rates. As a result property tax as a percentage of total tax revenue has declined from 8.1% in 1977 to 3.8%

in 1983. Similarly it was the middle class who benefited disproportionately from the uses to which the borrowed money was put – investment in infrastructure such as roads and telephones and increases in state subsidies for various services such as education or health care. Again, while the latter may also benefit the poor, studies done in Britain show that it is the rich and not the poor who benefit more from government spending.

In another very important way, the rich in Ireland continue to benefit from the national debt. With some 60% of the debt borrowed domestically, Irish investors have over recent years been able to charge high interest rates which the government, anxious to borrow their cash, had to pay. This is money lent at no risk whatsoever, yet it has been able to make up to 16% profit on the transaction due simply to government demand. In an article in *The Sunday Tribune*, columnist Paul Tansey estimated that the government paid IR£2bn to private financiers in 1987 alone as interest payments on the national debt, representing just under a quarter of total current government expenditure.

The final irony of the debt, however, is that it is the poor who are being forced to bear the brunt of paying back the debt. It is they who suffer most from cutbacks particularly in the health service. In an indirect way, they are also worst hit by the lack of government investment in job creation and in the economy generally. In this way, therefore, the national debt serves as a mechanism to redistribute wealth in favour of the already wealthy in our society and away from the poorest 40%.

The EEC

If domestic trends in Ireland point to a growing gap between rich and poor, similar trends have become obvious between the richer and poorer regions of the European Economic Community which Ireland joined in 1973. Though joining the EEC coincided with a period of increasing living standards for almost all in Western Europe, this cloaks the fact that the already rich regions grew faster than the poorer regions, of which Ireland is one. Both EEC and Irish studies have confirmed this trend.

One example is the National Economic and Social Council (NESC) report which showed that in the first seven years of membership, Ireland became poorer relative to the other EEC member states. While average income per person in Ireland was 65% of the EEC average in 1973, it had decreased to 61% by 1979. Meanwhile average income in West Germany had risen from 77% of the average in 1973 to 93% in 1979. Even the EEC Commission itself acknowledged this in a report published in 1980. As the report concluded: 'The underprivileged farm-worker of southern Italy or Ireland, the out-of-work miner or shipyard worker of Scotland. . . none of these will have an interest in a Community which seems to condemn them and their families to perpetual poverty as second class citizens.'[7]

As the addition of Greece, Spain and Portugal in the 1980s added to the poorer regions of the Community, the Commission's answer to the growing regional disparities has been to pledge increased regional and social funds. These have run into continuous difficulties within the European Council with some of the richer countries less than wholehearted in their support. However, a regional fund, even where it is generously funded and channelled to the regions of greatest poverty on the periphery of the Community, would function rather in the way that social welfare benefits function in the domestic Irish situation. Such payments might cushion the worst effects of poverty, but the actual trends themselves are towards ever widening disparities between rich and poor.

The Ecumenical Research Exchange in Rotterdam is an independent, church-funded research organisation which studies such trends in the EEC. In a report on the evolution of regional disparities in the Community, the ERE concluded that the underlying philosophy of the EEC and the policies being followed are responsible for these growing disparities:

The underlying [EEC] philosophy still seems to be based on a trust in free market forces as propounded by neo-classical economic theorists. The free market, however, has not proved able to restore the regional equilibrium, but has actually increased inequality. Its mechanism has led to a disintegration of major industries and regions in the Community, and created an inner and outer Europe of rich and poor countries. This mechanism is in fact neither universally efficient in achieving production of what is really needed by people nor generally capable of distributing either income or production with any pretence to even minimal standards of justice. If, in spite of experience to the contrary, free market forces are trusted by some to function in the direction of an equilibrium, this can only be interpreted as being ideological in nature and ought to be unmasked as that. . .[8]

In an interview in Dublin, one of the report's authors, Dr Wolf-Dieter Just, a West German Lutheran theologian, elaborated on these conclusions.

If a fragile, periphery economy is exposed to competition with a strong economy of the most developed EEC countries, then, of course, it is at a disadvantage. In our studies on the enlargement of the EEC, we have shown very clearly that this is going to have quite damaging effects on the small and medium-sized industries and firms in those [recent member] countries because they will not be able to stand up to European competition. Only the large firms and industries will survive and benefit from the enlarged market. And due to this concentration and rationalisation, there will be growing unemployment, the closure of many firms and the marginalisation of sectors of society like small farmers, small manufacturers and other social groups.[9]

For Dr Just, Ireland is an example of these consequences.

Yes, that seems to have happened in Ireland. Ireland is said to have benefited a lot from membership of the EEC, and this is true if one looks simply at the growth of GDP. But the important question which needs to be asked is *who* in Ireland has benefited and who has not. It seems that especially the large farmers have been able to benefit because the system of stabilised prices for agricultural products favours only those who produce a surplus.

The more surplus you produce, the more you benefit from these guaranteed prices. But farmers who exist more or less on subsistence level don't benefit.

Another factor that worries Dr Just and his colleagues is the growing concentration of power among the richer countries of the Community. In their report on regional disparities, they referred to this as a process of 'internal colonialism', through which the dominant countries impose socio-economic patterns of development and even cultural values on the weaker, poorer countries. Dr Just expanded on this growing concentration of wealth and power:

Due to the greater concentration and rationalisation taking place, due to the growing economic power of the richer countries and regions, their political power is also growing. In the peripheries [of the EEC], this trend has certainly destabilising effects. Unemployment rates are growing everywhere, but in the periphery they are growing faster than in the centre.

It is always the poor who have to pay the bill and who are most hard hit by the lack of job opportunities, by inflation, and by incentives being given to multinational capital, making a country attractive by keeping wages low. It is the poor who suffer from a situation where you have fierce competition with a very strong economic power. This is certainly having political effects also. Now, with an enlarged community, it is likely that there will be a few powers in the Community dominating the rest, some sort of directorates involving probably West Germany, France and perhaps Britain and Italy, which will dominate the rest of the Community. . . . In this situation, the rich countries will have a far better chance to get their way.

These trends, concentrating wealth and power in the already rich and powerful regions in the centre of the EEC and reducing the peripheral regions to greater poverty and dependence, have been strongly re-inforced by the Single European Act. This will eliminate all final barriers to a complete free market by the year 1992 thus further deepening the effects of open competition on the weaker peripheral economies, including Ireland. Furthermore, the SEA has weakened the practice whereby countries could veto any measure not in their national interest, thus strengthening the political power of the larger EEC countries. The end result looks set to deepen those divisions which the authors of the ERE report compared to the divisions between the First and the Third world:

> It has now become common to speak of an 'intra-European colonisation' which exhibits the typical problems of dependent development – foreign domination in economic and even political affairs, the dualism of local elites and poor masses, growing unemployment, declining social coherence, migrancy, illiteracy, poor housing conditions and health services, cultural alienation, abuse of religion as a tool to maintain the status quo, etc.[10]

Many will say that Ireland is not a poor country, and in comparison to the incomes of most of the world's people that is true. Per capita incomes in Ireland have increased dramatically over the past 30 years and it appears very unlikely that they could fall back to what they were then. But what cannot be denied are the trends which are marginalising more and more of our people from access to work and an income sufficient to meet their basic needs. These are the 'new oppressed' and their numbers are growing rapidly. These trends can be cushioned by higher social welfare benefits and greater charitable efforts, but they will not be changed by such means. They place a fundamental question mark over the direction in which Ireland is currently going, offering no hope for the future to so many of our young and not so young.

CHAPTER 2

Ireland in Crisis:
The Spiral of Violence

Just as we in Ireland inevitably see places like Central America and the Middle East as being synonymous with violence, so do many people throughout the world link Ireland with violence. Whether we like it or not, the past 20 years of violence and instability in the North have placed Ireland on the map of world trouble-spots. Though we might claim that the death toll of those 20 years has been small by comparison with other trouble-spots, Northern Ireland compares with some of the more notorious when the level of militarisation, the counter-insurgency campaign of the security forces, the persistence and extent of guerrilla actions or the human rights abuses by the authorities are compared.

Despite this, however, the reaction of most Irish people is the wholehearted wish that the problem would simply disappear. Deeply confused by what is happening, public opinion in the Republic constantly reacts to the latest atrocity. When this is perpetrated by the IRA, condemnation is focused on them. At moments like the verdict on the Birmingham Six or the British government's decision not to prosecute RUC officers implicated in an alleged shoot-to-kill policy, public opinion seems dramatically to swing into momentary anti-British moods. These, however, last only until the next IRA atrocity. The result is that an atrocity like the Enniskillen bombing can change overnight what seemed a growing consensus against extradition in the Republic.

Many expressed the hope that Enniskillen might mark a decisive turning point in the Northern 'troubles'. Playwright Frank McGuinness eloquently expressed the widely felt desperation and revulsion:

For the sins of the fathers revenge has been taken against the children of Enniskillen. From the day of this bombing they will date their lives. That is the legacy bestowed upon them. They in turn will bestow theirs on us, making us all children of Enniskillen, stumbling together through this island, crawling forward through the mess of our history, living and dying in a house that is now forever divided. All is changed after Enniskillen.[1]

For all the tears shed and the prayers said, for all the eloquent condemnations and the earnest pleas for peace, however, Enniskillen changed nothing. Amid all these what was obvious was the widespread lack of any thorough reflection on the roots of the problem. Award-winning *Irish Times* columnist Nuala O'Faolain was one of the few who identified this need at the time:

> I think that most people here would heartily wish that all the troubles would go away, or stay quiet, and stop costing us money and self-esteem and self-confidence, stop splitting and confusing and hurting us, stop dragging us down. . . Condemning the violence is altogether right, but it is only the easiest option unless we take that condemnation as the beginning of a period of honest talking and thinking which will in some way help us to deal with this situation.[2]

Without such honest talking and thinking, nothing is really going to change.

Understanding violence

In terms of political violence, Ireland can be likened to parts of Latin America. There the phenomenon has given rise to a serious attempt to understand it and to identify its real causes. One of the first people to attempt such an analysis was the former Archbishop Helder Camara of Recife in Brazil. He coined the term 'spiral of violence' to describe the way in which violence begets more violence, a spiral which is all too visible in Ireland over recent years. But the archbishop also resisted the temptation simply to condemn the more visible manifestations of that violence, namely violence used as a means to achieve political change. Instead, in his book *Spiral of Violence*, he identified three forms of violence, all of which can be clearly seen to be operative in the Irish situation.

The first and most basic violence identified by Camara is the pervasive injustice present in societies throughout the world. 'There exists very often what could be called a heritage of poverty: It is common knowledge that poverty kills just as surely as the most bloody war. . . You will find that everywhere the injustices are a form of violence. One can and must say that they are everywhere the basic violence, violence Number One.'[3] The second violence he identifies is the revolt against these injustices. This too applies to Ireland. 'Violence attracts violence. Let us repeat fearlessly and ceaselessly: injustices bring revolt, either from the oppressed or from the young, determined to fight for a more just and more human world,' writes Camara.[4] Finally, comes the repressive violence of the state. 'When conflict comes out into the streets, when violence Number Two tries to resist violence Number One, the authorities consider themselves obliged to preserve or re-establish public order, even if this means using force; this is violence Number Three. Sometimes they go even further, and this is becoming increasingly common: in order to obtain information, which may indeed be important to public security, the logic of violence leads them to use moral and physical torture,' he says.[5]

Archbishop Camara is not alone in this understanding of violence. Archbishop Oscar Romero of San Salvador, himself a victim of state violence, developed this understanding in a long pastoral letter he wrote in August 1979. Entitled *The Mission of the Church amid the Country's Crisis*, he devoted nine paragraphs to the question of violence. The late archbishop begins by reflecting on the criteria to be used in judging violence.

> The peace the church seeks to realise is the work of justice. Because of this, its judgements about that form of violence which disturbs the peace cannot neglect the demands of justice. The judgements it makes are very different according to the different

forms violence takes, in such a way that the church cannot affirm, in a simplistic manner, that it simply condemns all forms of violence.[6]

Knowing that a blanket condemnation of violence often cloaks a refusal to analyse its roots and understand from where it comes, Romero goes on to distinguish six forms of violence. The first of these is 'structural violence'. 'More and more people in this country are becoming aware,' he writes, 'that the ultimate root of the serious problems afflicting us, including the outbreak of violence, is this "structural violence" expressed in the unjust distribution of wealth and property. . . and, in general, in that aggregate of economic and political structures as a result of which the few become ever more rich and powerful while the rest become ever more poor and weak.'

Out of this fundamental violence, different expressions of violence arise. Romero gives pride of place to 'arbitrary state violence' used to repress 'whatever dissent arises against the present form of capitalism and its political institutionalisation.' The 'violence of the extreme right,' he goes on, 'tries to maintain the unjust social order to which I have referred above.' The next form of violence condemned by the late archbishop is 'unjust terrorist violence' which he defines as the violence of 'politico-military groups' which 'intentionally causes innocent victims or results disproportionate to the positive effect which it is hoped to achieve in the short or medium term.'

While Romero condemns all these forms of violence, he then goes on to mention two forms which can be legitimate. The first is 'insurrectionary violence' and he quotes Pope Paul VI who reaffirmed the classical Catholic teaching that 'in the very exceptional case of evident and prolonged tyranny' this form of violence is legitimate.[7] Finally, he mentions the 'violence of legitimate defence, when a person or group repel by force an unjust aggression to which they have been subjected.'[8]

Romero, however, is not content simply to mention such

forms of violence which can be legitimate. In a further paragraph he sets out three conditions: firstly, that defensive violence is not greater than the aggression against which it is addressed; secondly, that resort is had to violence only after all peaceful means have been exhausted and, thirdly, that the use of violence does not lead to a worse wrong than the one it is designed to eliminate. He then adds that history teaches us 'how cruel and sad is the price of blood'. Better, he urges, that governments use their power 'not to defend the structural violence of an unjust order but to guarantee a truly democratic state and to defend the fundamental rights of all citizens based on a just social order.'

Violence in Northern Ireland

Any attempt to understand the spiral of violence engulfing Northern Ireland must begin with the fundamental violence out of which it has grown. Borrowing from Archbishop Romero, the term 'institutionalised violence' accurately describes the plight of much of the Nationalist community in the way they have been treated by the state and society in Northern Ireland. The permanent discrimination through which Nationalists were excluded from political power and employment shocked British public opinion when it came to international attention as a result of the Civil Rights Movement in the late 1960s. Reforms were quickly enacted in an attempt to ensure for Nationalists equal access to power and wealth in Northern Ireland. What is unfortunate about the subsequent history of the North, with its concentration on the paramilitary groups of both communities, is the failure to appreciate just how much this institutionalised violence remains a daily experience for the working class Nationalist community.

It is disturbing in the extreme to find that, after almost 20 years of imposed reforms by Westminster, Catholics are still two and a half times more likely to be unemployed than are Protestants and that Protestant households enjoy a substantially better standard of living than do Catholic ones.

These are the main results of a major two-year study carried out for the Standing Advisory Committee on Human Rights (SACHR) in Northern Ireland by the London-based Policy Studies Institute and published at the end of October 1987. It found, for example, that 50% or more of Protestant households had nine or more out of a list of 18 consumer items such as television, hi-fi or video while only 32% of Catholic households attained this level. What is perhaps most significant about this particular study is that it rules out causes other than discrimination on religious grounds for the large disparities it uncovered. 'We conclude that after allowing for all factors that are known to be relevant and important, religion is a major determinant of the rate of unemployment,' it says.[9]

Based on this study, the state-sponsored SACHR recommended as a goal to be achieved by 1992 that Protestants would be only one and a half times more likely to be in employment. Without such urgent action, it said, the sense of grievance in the Catholic community would grow. In the context of the history of the Northern Ireland state, such a bland comment amounts to an almost ludicrous understatement of the extent of alienation among the Nationalist community. This, the legacy of deeply-rooted institutionalised violence, will continue to be reinforced as long as the situation highlighted by the report lasts.

What such a report also underlines, however, is just how difficult it is to reform the Northern Ireland state and society in such a way as to ensure equality of treatment and opportunity for all. If the apparent efforts of successive London governments over 20 years have failed to evoke greater confidence in Northern Ireland and its institutions among much of the Nationalist community, on what can one base a real hope that such efforts will succeed in future?

Just as the roots of the present-day problems lie in this institutionalised violence, they have been aggravated by the next two forms of violence identified by Archbishop Romero. It was the state violence meeted out to the peaceful protests of the Civil Rights Movement in 1968 and 1969 that began the so-called 'Troubles'. The reasons for such arbitrary state violence can partly be described in Romero's words: 'to repress. . . whatever dissent against the actual form of capitalism and its political institutionalisation.'[10]

By summer 1969, Nationalist housing estates in West Belfast experienced 'the violence of the extreme right' as they were attacked by Loyalist mobs backed up by the RUC and B-Specials. These, using Romero's analysis, were 'seeking to maintain the unjust social order'. This form of violence has continued in the sectarian attacks by Loyalist paramilitary groups.

Soon the British army, welcomed by the Nationalists as their defenders when they first arrived in August 1969, also began to be used to maintain the institutionalised violence of the Northern Ireland state. The key turning point was the curfew imposed on the Falls Road in Belfast in July 1970 when the army carried out a systematic search of homes in the area for IRA arms. Meanwhile Loyalist areas, from where almost all the active violence had originated, were left untouched.

While the nature of the harassment suffered by the Nationalist community has changed with the ebb and flow of the political and security situation over recent years, it remains as an ever-present reality particularly in working class areas. The extent of such harassment is clearly demonstrated on occasions such as the allegedly accidental killing by a British soldier of the young Catholic Aidan McAnespie at a border post in February 1988. Only after his death was it discovered that he had been harassed by the security forces for the previous two years. For the small number of such cases that capture the public limelight, it is obvious that such harassment is a regular experience in many working class Catholic areas. It is just one example of the ways in which the arbitrary counter-violence of the state remains a constant irritant, aggravating the sense of alienation deeply felt by many Northern Catholics.

This situation of institutionalised violence, protected by the counter-violence of the state, was eloquently summed up by Fr Raymond Murray of Armagh in an article in the summer 1988 issue of *Resource* magazine:

> British government policy is to keep Ireland weak and keep the nationalists of the north particularly weak. The campaign of nationalists for justice has been met with such state violence as to cause the rebirth and continuance of the IRA. The violence of the state has resulted in awful short-term problems for nationalists and here you have a plethora of injustices – internment, harassment, torture, inhuman and degrading treatment, severe prison conditions, strip-searching, corrupt courts, informers, blackmail, extradition, unjust killing and 'Shoot to Kill'. The political and legal rights of citizens in Northern Ireland are being violated on an extensive scale; this has been systematic and persistent over twenty years. The British government controls the situation and condones such violations. Indeed it has been directly responsible for the injustices, employing police-state tactics as a matter of official, if unannounced, policy.

The IRA/Sinn Féin

The origins of the Provisional IRA can also be situated within the analysis as developed by Archbishop Romero. For, he saw that the victims of arbitrary state violence 'have often been seen to be obliged to defend themselves, even in violent forms.' During the August 1969 progroms, the people taunted the few remnants of the 1952-62 IRA campaign by painting on walls 'IRA – I Ran Away'. Even the Scarman Tribunal, which investigated the events of the summer of 1969 for the British government, admitted that the IRA had a minor part in them and did less than many local people might have wanted.

It was only as a result of this violence, and largely as a defence for the Nationalist areas, that the IRA became active again. Their arms were still very primitive and it was not until February 1971 that the first British soldier was killed. Anybody thought to be associated with the IRA or even a potential recruit became a target for the security forces, so much so that Tim Pat Coogan in his book *Disillusioned Decades* quotes a Special Branch officer in the Republic as saying: 'The Army created the IRA.'[11]

In examining the situation in Northern Ireland, therefore, it is important to realise that the Provisional IRA (or breakaway groups from them like the INLA or the more recent IPLO) are not the cause of the present violence. Neither would the ending of their campaigns put an end to all political violence in Northern Ireland though that would certainly lessen it. The more fundamental institutionalised violence of the state and society still exists, somewhat modified since the late 1960s but still very pervasive. And the arbitrary violence of the security forces and right-wing paramilitary bands, continues to aggravate the situation.

To say this, however, is not to justify the armed campaign of those groups committed to changing the situation. Apart from a purely defensive role against attacks by Loyalist mobs, it is difficult to see any justification for a campaign of violence which itself has been a major factor in polarising community divisions and, in some ways, aggravating the situation of the Nationalist minority itself. While it has helped to uncover the sectarian nature of the Northern Ireland state, it is difficult to see how it has brought any closer its final demise.

None of the three criteria outlined by Archbishop Romero to justify the use of violence to change a situation, appear to be fulfilled in the conditions of Northern Ireland today, i.e. that the defensive violence is not greater than the aggression, that all peaceful means have been exhausted and that the use of violence does not lead to worse problems. Finally, the greatest successes of the IRA/Sinn Féin have come about, not as a result of armed actions, but of developing a political strategy. The hunger strikes, and especially the election of Bobby Sands, marked what was the movement's high point. Far more successfully than all its armed struggle, it succeeded in undermining the moral authority of the British in the eyes of the world. However there are those, clergy included, who would see the IRA's armed struggle as morally legitimate.

The underlying weakness of the IRA/Sinn Féin is political. While they compare themselves to liberation movements in Third World situations, the enormous difference is that such liberation movements, whether it is the ANC in South Africa, the FMLN in El Salvador or the NPA in the Philippines, have all grown out of a sophisticated political movement. The resort to violence in each case came only after a mass movement with a developed political consciousness was well established as a major actor on the political stage. In each country, the armed struggle is seen as a regrettable result of the closing off of all possible political avenues for change.

In the Sinn Féin/IRA case, however, the development has been, if anything, the opposite. The Provisional IRA did not grow out of a developed political movement but rather out of the immediate defensive needs of sectors of the Nationalist community. It took many years for Sinn Féin to emerge as a serious political movement in its own right. As a result, the movement's political outlook is still relatively undeveloped, no matter how much the present leadership may like to think otherwise. Even most IRA recruits still appear to be motivated more by a resentment of the security forces than by any wider political strategy. To merit comparison with Third World liberation movements, Sinn Féin still has a long way to go in developing a sophisticated political consciousness among its rank and file membership and translating this into a credible strategy to achieve their stated goal of a thirty-two county democratic socialist republic.

Meanwhile, political attitudes in the Republic are far from helpful in facilitating any real solution to the northern impasse. Public opinion vacillates between sympathy for the IRA at a time like Derry's Bloody Sunday in January 1972 or the hunger strikes of 1980-81 while resorting to absolute condemnations of the movement, and even of republicanism itself, at times like the Enniskillen bombing. Underlying such vacillation is the fact that the institutionalised violence of Northern society is quickly forgotten as the root cause of the problem.

Meanwhile the fundamental aspiration for a united Ireland as the only possible context for a solution is relegated to the realm of the unattainable. Attempts to find a way out of this impasse, such as the New Ireland Forum and the subsequent Anglo-Irish Agreement, have yet to show themselves able to change the fundamental sectarianism of the Northern state. The final hypocrisy of this national confusion is Section 31 which does not allow IRA or Sinn Féin spokespersons be interviewed on RTÉ, thereby excusing them of the need to justify their actions to the Irish public.

Ireland's Protestant (Unionist) minority

Central to the impasse that prevents any real breakthrough in the Northern Ireland situation is the Protestant ascendency. Though constituting a majority within the Northern statelet, their fundamental fear of change betrays the siege mentality that is the hallmark of the threatened minority they really are. The Northern Presbyterian clergyman, Robert G. Crawford, describes in his book *Loyal to King Billy* their captivity to a history of superiority:

> This is true of both their politics and their religion. That bigotry, intolerance, narrow-mindedness, tribalism, defensiveness, sectarianism, arrogance, siege-mentality, prejudice, obstinacy, fear, sense of grievance – all spring from this captivity to the past. What is required is a change of mentality.[12]

Irish history has left no sadder legacy than this historically trapped community. The sadness of their fate is particularly poignant when one appreciates the many wonderful qualities that characterise so many Northern Protestants – their kindness, their thrift and hard work, their energy and, as was so eloquently testified by the remarkable response of so many relatives of victims of the Enniskillen bombing, the depth and strength of their christian faith.

As observers of some of the more public and offensive manifestations of Northern Protestantism, we can often overlook its positive traits. Unfortunately, however, the particular historical circumstances of economic superiority in which Irish Protestantism developed, led to the development of a theological and political outlook which blinds many of its adherents to the urgent need for social and political change.

The nearest equivalent to the theology of Northern Protestantism is that of South Africa's Afrikaners. Both are colonial communities who have inhabited the land for about 400 years. Two factors have determined the development of their distinctive theology – their Calvinist background and their situation as beleaguered minorities surrounded by hostile peoples. For both, historical victories over these peoples constitute the fundamental experiences that underpin their sense of superiority. For Northern Protestants, the key victory was the Battle of the Boyne while the victory over the Zulus at Blood River in 1838 constitutes a similar key element in the identity of the Afrikaners.

Born out of this is a common certainty of being God's chosen people, assured of prevailing over their enemies who surround them. Both seek to maintain their economic and political superiority through separation from those they consider a threat – the blacks in South Africa and Catholics (Nationalists) in the Irish case. It is no accident that mixed marriage constitutes a major act of treachery for both as it threatens the purity and, in the long run, even the very survival of this 'chosen race.' Both have their elitist organisations, dedicated to the survival of their supremacy – the Orange Order in the North and the Broederbond in South Africa.

While the underlying theology (it is, of course, more strictly an ideology of racial superiority masquerading as christian theology) shows these similarities, perhaps more significant are the policies followed by both groups in an attempt to prevent any threat to their superiority. Thus apartheid involves not just a separation of the races but ultimately the attempt to constitute an artificial white majority by dividing the black population and relegating them to the *bantustans* or homelands. This policy could then give the facade of 'democracy' to white supremacy as it eliminates any basis for the blacks to claim power in white South Africa.

The partition of Ireland involved a similar logic. When faced with the inevitability of an Irish state emerging in which the majority would dominate political power, Irish Unionists opted to create an artificial state where they could perpetuate their supremacy under the guise of being a majority. All attempts to wrest that supremacy from them are consequently met with an appeal by Unionist leaders to their democratic rights. It is possible to envisage that if the white minority in South Africa had introduced their *bantustan* policy 30 or 40 years ago, they too would probably now be resisting black demands for a share in the country's wealth and opportunities by referring to the white 'majority's' democratic rights.

Attempts to reform both societies and give the majority peoples a share in political power and its benefits have also run along similar lines. Both Northern Ireland and South Africa have proved very resistant to giving their excluded peoples a share in power. As these peoples demanded such a share with ever greater insistence, the previously monolithic power structure splintered with significant results. In South Africa, the ruling National Party saw ultra-right factions break away in protest at any reform of apartheid while, in the North, the attempts of liberals within the Unionist Party to share power with the SDLP led to a similar splintering and the emergence of the more right-wing Loyalist groups, particularly the DUP.

In both countries also, those more liberal elements who genuinely sought an end to the structure of supremacy through peaceful reform found themselves with little electoral support. This is as true of Brian Faulkner's Unionist Party of Northern Ireland or of the Alliance Party as it is of the Progressive Federal Party in South Africa. Similarly, various Labour parties in both Northern Ireland and South Africa, seeking to avoid the sectarian or racial issue and instead campaign for social democratic reforms, have met with little success.

Underlying the failure of most whites in South Africa or the

Unionists of Northern Ireland even to consider meaningful and far-reaching reform is the sense of threat both feel. This is deeply rooted in the history and psyche of both peoples, making them unable to consider their political situation in any rational way and instead leading them to take refuge in their siege mentality, determined to hold out against the tide they fear is about to engulf them.

Both remain impervious to the most elaborate of guarantees that any real sharing of power will not lead to their extinction. Instead they hold on doggedly to what they have. As the Rev Crawford, who himself lived in South Africa, says:

> Certainly the right-wing Afrikaners and ultra-loyalist Ulster Protestants have apparently unassailable reasons for what they do and say, but in the democratic Western world they seem an anachronism. Their theology and politics have not advanced with the times, and their history, instead of being a blessing, has become a burden. The burden is likely to become heavier as time goes on.[13]

Any examination of the political and psychological situation of Northern Unionists leads to grave doubts that any significant reform of the Northern Ireland state is possible. The painful events of the last 20 years seem to confirm such a conclusion. Indeed, the very existence of the northern statelet, set up as it was to perpetuate Protestant supremacy, acts to fuel the siege mentality of the Unionist population.

Reconciliation between the different traditions or identities on this island is the stated aim of the main churches and most of the political parties. Reconciliation is, however, a far more painful and far-reaching process than is usually acknowledged. Far from involving simply that we all learn to live with each other, it must involve a recognition of the wrongs we have committed against each other in the past and an attempt to discover new ways of relating for the future. Such a process demands facing the hard facts of historical supremacy and victimisation so as to destroy the structures which perpetuate them. Southern Catholics are often rightly told that such a process must involve their questioning Catholic laws and dominance in the Republic. But for Northern Protestants also, profound soul-searching is needed.

There are already signs that the resolve of the British government in maintaining its support for the Anglo-Irish Agreement is forcing Unionist leaders to begin such a soul-searching. Both the Unionist Task Force Report and the UDA's 'Common Sense' document have indicated some movement in the Unionist leadership. A willingness to consider talks with the Republic's government also shows such movement.

Such movement may eventually lead the Unionists to confront their own history and acknowledge their responsibility for the Northern situation. It might even help them to discover those more radical strands in the northern Presbyterian tradition, dating back to the United Irishmen and, later, to the liberal theology of Henry Montgomery in the early part of the last century. Such a tradition has much to offer us all.

An over-exclusive emphasis on the North or even on Ireland as a whole, in the search for a solution, is not sufficient either. Britain's role over the past 20 years and its growing, and at times exclusive, emphasis on security alerts us to the fact that more than conflicting identities is at stake in Northern Ireland. Security of a wider kind also appears to be at stake, with the apparent fear in the minds of some members of the British establishment that a united Ireland could become a European 'Cuba'. As Fr Raymond Murray put it in the article of his already quoted:

> Ireland was conquered by Britain because it was a back-door to possible invasion of Britain, an idea accentuated by wars with Spain, France and Germany. But one asks – is it necessary now in the age of missiles and 'star wars'? The answer seems to be 'Yes'. One feels that the United States would not tolerate an independent neutral Ireland.

This wider, and perhaps crucial, aspect of the Northern Ireland problem needs far more attention.

The violence and instability of Northern Ireland cannot be

thought of by people in the Republic as a distant problem of little immediate concern to them. For it continues to act as an obstacle to the development of this island as a whole, diverting resources to the security forces and justifying growing police powers and surveillance in both parts of the island. It serves to distract attention and political energies from the urgent social and economic problems of north and south and deeply divides the left which should be providing an alternative. It casts a shadow over all plans and hopes for the future of Ireland.

CHAPTER 3

Ireland in Crisis: An Alienated Society

What is most disturbing about contemporary Ireland is not the extent of our problems. Problems such as economic decline, mass unemployment, growing crime, a huge national debt and high levels of political violence we share with many of the world's countries, particularly those of the Third World. In comparison to many, our problems are relatively manageable. But what is extremely disturbing is our reluctance to face these problems in any thorough way, our apparent paralysis in fashioning radical and humane responses.

Instead of a sense of struggle, one encounters a passivity and paralysis among people all too aware that we face serious problems but lacking the human resources to confront them. Instead of hope, one encounters an all-pervasive sense of depression and hopelessness among people who cannot any longer even imagine a better future. Disillusioned with the false and empty promises of successive political leaders and unable to find any other basis on which to ground their hopes, many lapse into quiet despair. In this situation, emigration becomes the only avenue of escape and many experience it as a liberation, renewing their sense of life.

This malaise at the heart of Irish life is no passing phenomenon. While the country's economic and social problems of the 1980s, and the particular austerity policies chosen to combat them, may add to the sense of despair, its roots lie far deeper. Underlying our paralysis, is an inability to name this malaise, to identify it, to analyse its causes and to combat it. Our media reflects a smug and complacent society with little self-questioning and no challenges to the prevailing orthodoxy. Our voting and church-going patterns continue to portray a society of remarkable stability as radically shifting economic and cultural patterns over the past 25 years have largely eroded the foundations of that stability.

Indeed so marked has the gap become between the dominant institutions of Irish society and the values, lifestyles, expectations and needs of large sectors of the population that these institutions themselves act as a kind of straitjacket further adding to the widespread sense of alienation. This is particularly true of the Catholic church and of our main political parties, whose restricted and narrow visions hamper any wider release of creative energies.

Alienation

Alienation is a term we usually apply in a very restricted sense. We speak of the alienation of Northern Catholics or of the alienating nature of many modern housing estates. In its deeper sense, however, it is a term that aptly describes the malaise many Irish people feel today as aliens in their own society, lacking any ability to identify either with what it is or with what it could become.

Particularly among more deprived sectors of the population, what is frighteningly obvious is the final breakdown of those age-old structures of family solidarity and community bonds on which all societies depend for survival. High levels of teenage drug abuse and violence point to this breakdown, telling symbols of very extreme alienation from present-day Irish society which cannot offer even the most minor role to these young people.

Many women feel deeply alienated in a society which can so freely use seductive female images to market its goods. Many of our parties, our dances, even our liturgical celebrations express feelings of alienation. Instead of being life-enhancing they are all too often life-negating, either frenzied escapes from reality or the bored acting out of roles. A general inability to feel good about ourselves and our society, a widespread inability to affirm our present or our future direction, characterise Irish life today.

Contemporary Ireland is not unique in displaying various forms of alienation. The very structures of urban life itself, the dizzying impact of contemporary technology, the widening gap between rich and poor which characterise all developed capitalist societies, are factors we share with many other peoples. But these do not excuse us from the urgent task of looking searchingly at ourselves in order to identify those many unique factors which generate such high levels of alienation in Irish culture.

Dr Ivor Browne is one of our few public figures who has sought to do this. He says that 'Ireland is not a well nation', and points out that studies have shown that there are between three and five times as many mental patients in Irish mental hospitals as in Britain. He goes further, however, and identifies characteristics of mental illness in our culture:

> Everyone in this country is subject in greater or lesser degree to the apathy, helplessness and loss of autonomy born of oppression. It is no use, however fashionable, to say that this oppression is behind us. It is seen most clearly in our unawareness of personal responsibility and in our unawareness of the possibility of our potential as a people and as persons Our past as a nation has been so crushing and so painful that we are too inclined to rush blindly ahead and leave it behind us. The fact is, that we cannot go ahead in any real sense unless we can identify where we are in relation to where we have been. Who are we now? What sort of a society are we prepared to put our backs into? Or are we only concerned with aping our oppressors, with proving to ourselves that we are the same as they were and can use the same methods of oppression on each other. After fifty years of independence we are still afraid to cast off the security of oppression. But our fear of freedom, our inability to believe in ourselves is costing us dearly.[1]

This is the legacy of colonialism, a legacy we share with all post-colonial societies. Indeed, for few peoples was colonisation such a profoundly destructive historical experience as it was for the Irish, obliterating our own civilisation and its institutions, uprooting us from the land and leaving us communicating with each other through the language of the coloniser. As Dr Browne emphasises in his description, in our refusal as a people to acknowledge and come to terms with that history lies the roots of the apathy and powerlessness that so strongly characterise us today. These block us from facing our present and from tackling the tasks ahead with vigour and creativity.

A sense of identity is crucial for each individual's self-realisation. Human growth and development can be described as the process of discovering one's identity – coming to terms with one's family past, recognising one's strengths and weaknesses, finding the ability to relate to others as an equal and uncovering the sources of one's own creativity.

National identity is no less important yet our traditional obsession with the notion of our separate identity is itself a sign of just how little we have really discovered ourselves. We have already this century had two separate identities imposed upon us, both of which we seem to have accepted with relative resignation. De Valera's Gaelic, Catholic and Nationalist Ireland, made up of frugal homesteads and comely maidens, gave way overnight to the new pluralist, European and technological Ireland, embarrassed at its nationalist past and frantically trying to show our EEC 'partners' that we are as sophisticated as they are. The relative ease with which we passed from one to the other, symbolised by the nationalist Fianna Fáil painlessly becoming the champion of multinational capitalism, itself shows that neither set of images expresses anything essential we feel about ourselves.

Few of us identify in any deep way with the Irish people or with the piece of land we inhabit together. As a consequence we recognise no common experience upon which to reflect, no common future for which to struggle, no bonds of solidarity with one another. Any thorough probing of what is actually happening on and to this island would quickly develop class consciousness as workers, small farmers and the growing masses of the marginalised would begin to identify with one another in challenging the social project of the dominant elites.

Instead, the lack of class consciousness is itself a symptom of our failure to discover any identity based on who we really are. Most workers still vote for Fianna Fáil rather than for any party whose policies would, however mildly, favour them and seek to impose restraints on capital. Small farmers are fast committing suicide as a class because they identify with large farmers in whose interest it is to get rid of them. As Desmond Fennell has written, 'a feeling of paralysis is lying heavily on people and national purpose is palpably absent'.[2]

The two referenda: amorality

Every now and again things come to the surface of Irish life which remind us that the new pseudo-sophisticated identity of the pluralist, developed and secular Ireland lies very lightly upon us. The referenda of 1983, on adding a so-called pro-life clause to the constitution, and of 1986, on divorce were two such moments in our recent past.

The Ireland they revealed shocked many who had taken it for granted that the old Catholic orthodoxy was fast being replaced by more secular and pluralist views. Interpreted as a conflict between enlightened liberalism and reactionary Catholicism, many were forced to conclude that change was going to come far more slowly than they had anticipated. For those on the winning side in both contests, there was a sense that the liberal tide had been stopped in its tracks and that the majority had decisively spoken.

While the two referenda were very revealing, what they revealed was rather more complex than either side acknowledged. Both purported to be about moral issues but in fact what they showed up was the profound moral illiteracy and insensitivity of Irish society. For little of the professed concern about morality, expressed with such passion during the contests, ever seems to be applied in Ireland to anything other than sex-related issues. Certainly, many of those publicly associated with the referenda, particularly those who loudly profess their 'pro-life' stance, are not seen to express such passionate concern about the immorality of unemployment, homelessness or the treatment of Travellers. We still await such crusading vigour to be applied to amending the rights private property enjoys in our constitution or to adding a clause enshrining our neutrality in the basic law.

Such selective moral indignation as the referenda revealed gives grounds for suspicion about just how moral we are as a people. Dr Dolores Dooley, a UCC lecturer in philosophy, has written of what she calls 'the Irish "sense" of ethics which has dominated most of the last century.'[3] Focused on sexual issues and continually reinforced by family, pulpit and school, she writes, 'the net effect of this narrow focus in morality was that ethics became isolated from most areas of Irish public life: business, farming, politics, journalism, legal affairs, health-care, education: all insulated from moral scrutiny and relieved of the burdens of social accountability.'[4]

But if professed moral concern came to focus exclusively on sex, even in this area no true sense of morality and sensitivity to values were cultivated. In its place was taught a sort of ethical dogmatism, a set of rights and wrongs that people dared not question. Behind this facade of sexual propriety and uprightness lurks a hypocritical denial of facts such as the thousands of Irish women who go to England for abortions every year. Beneath the surface of sexual morality lies a lot of deeply repressed sexual feeling and pain. If our much professed concern about sexual morality was in any way a concern about real morality, then it would seek to face such important aspects of the problem instead of simply ignoring them.

What passes for morality in Ireland is far from moral. As Dr Dooley says: 'Ireland, over the last one-hundred years, reinforced a national morality which is largely monolithic and has remained so by being carefully insulated from alien challenges.'[5] This national morality, much proclaimed and constantly reinforced, lost touch with the real lived experience of people and has therefore been unable to develop shared authentic moral values. Rather than developing a true moral sensitivity, its real role seems to have been to provide a code of easy certainties insulating people from the ongoing challenge of fashioning values.

Dr Dooley writes that 'the traditional ethic has yet to show that its promise of certainty is not an illusion. The promise of certainty which offers such comfort may, in the end, be more of a consoling refuge than a constructive resource!'[6] What the 1983 and 1986 referenda showed, far more than any real concern for morality, was that sizeable minorities of the Irish people (since the total turnout was only slightly over half the electorate in both cases and the winning side represented less than 40% of it) still cling to such a consoling refuge. The self-righteous passion with which a small elite championed their so-called pro-life amendment and the deep fissures it opened in the Irish psyche seemed to have far more to do with deep insecurity than with moral concern.

A shabby and insecure amorality, masquerading as moral righteousness, stands revealed by the two referenda. They showed, as Dr Dooley has said, the need for school programmes 'encouraging skills of moral reasoning for reflection in a wide range of applied ethics: legal, corporation, medical, environment, industrial relations, economic ethics – all providing potential material for moral intelligence and imagination.'[7] The need for such programmes has been widely recognised by educators in recent years and various attempts made to develop them. Usually grouped under the term 'Life-skills', they are now in use in perhaps three-quarters of all post-primary schools in the country. The Health Education Bureau, before its abolition, provided training courses for teachers in Life-skills and the North Western Health Board and North Tipperary VEC have developed courses for all post-primary schools in their areas.

The aim of Life-skills is to help students develop the ability to make value choices in an environment of conflicting values. Traditional techniques for teaching values concentrated on telling students what was right and wrong and involved no training enabling them to internalise the values being taught.

Life-skills therefore uses methods of role-play, small-group discussion and problem-posing techniques to clarify by what values the student actually lives, allowing them critically to examine such values in the light of the value system espoused by family, school, church and society. Evaluations of the programmes currently in use indicate that both teachers and parents enthusiastically endorse them.

In the light of the professed concerns of those champions of morality in the 1983 and 1986 referenda, one could have expected that such moral education would have been welcomed by them. The opposite has been the case, however. A growing conservative lobby, including individuals and organisations active in the two referenda, has mounted a vigorous campaign against them, accusing them of being value-free and of undermining christian morality.

These voices espouse a return to traditional methods of teaching children right and wrong and claim that priests, sisters and brothers who teach Life-skills are in some way being duped by a secular-humanist plot. Despite the widespread support for Life-skills among teachers and parents, this campaign has succeeded in casting Life-skills in a certain disreputable light with the result that teachers using the programme feel they have to be on their guard against intimidation by some organisations.

The Life-skills controversy is disturbing. It confirms the deep sense of insecurity felt by certain sectors of Irish society about any move away from traditional moral codes. It is also disturbing as it shows that, far from any concern about real moral development, these sectors simply refuse to acknowledge the amorality of Irish life and the urgent need for programmes to foster more humane values in Irish society. Their own insecurity and inability to cope with any change leads them to deny the amoral reality around them.

The moving statues: fundamentalism

Another phenomenon in recent years that showed us elements of ourselves we would much prefer not to have to face were the moving statues. These were significant not so much for themselves as for their impact on Irish society. Our Lady has been reported to have moved in other parts of the world in recent years (in Spain and Yugoslavia) but only in Ireland did the reported movements become a major national event. To concentrate on whether or not the statues actually moved is to miss the most important point about it all. Even if it could be scientifically shown that they had moved, more important was the deep chord touched off in the Irish psyche by the whole phenomenon.

The reaction to the moving statues, the need that so many people apparently had to assure themselves that something supernatural was happening, alerts us to a deep spiritual crisis beneath the surface of Irish life. For, while the widespread interest showed that many Irish people still cling to their christian faith, it also showed that they need concrete manifestations to confirm them in that faith. Unable to cope with the widespread cultural challenge to faith in Irish society today, they seek 'signs and wonders' to convince themselves.

Commentators at the time expressed themselves surprised at the fact that so many luke-warm Catholics, hardened sceptics, or even self-proclaimed agnostics, were attracted to one of the many shrines. Yet this is hardly surprising since people with a mature and developed faith will be the first to be sceptical about such phenomena. Instead of needing the bizarre to confirm their faith, such believers find a sense of God in the everyday things of life.

As one letter writer to the Irish newspapers at the height of the reported Marian movements wrote of one of the shrines:

> Ballinspittle shows that much Irish religion is not. . . a personal conviction about the meaning of life and the power of love. . . but a frenzied chasing after supernatural kicks, based on a feared God of external power and tricks. . . Perhaps Ballinspittle shows us the underlying spiritual vacuum of much Catholicism?

As could be expected, the moving statues spectacle vanished as suddenly as it had made its appearance. This fact alone would tend to confirm that it expressed little that was genuinely religious. But the underlying psychological need lives on as can be seen in the large numbers of Irish people who travel to Medjugorje in Yugoslavia where Our Lady is also reported to appear every day.

The Medjugorje phenomenon is interesting for two reasons. Unlike Lourdes or Knock, to which Irish pilgrims also flock, in Medjugorje visitors hope to be present at an appearance of Our Lady though they know they will not be able to see anything. Such a promise cannot be offered by any other Marian shrine. Secondly, they go despite the scepticism of the local bishop who has submitted an unfavourable report to Rome on the phenomenon. There is in Medjugorje, therefore, something of the same need to confirm a faith under threat as there was in the moving statues, a need strong enough to defy official ecclesiastical scepticism.

Underlying these phenomena is a religious funda-mentalism. On the surface the commitment to peace emphasised in the devotions at Medjugorje is a worthy aspiration. Yet as an English priest, Fr Gerard W Hughes, wrote following a visit he paid to the shrine, this commitment can co-exist with strangely unpeaceful attitudes. 'Among some charismatics and devotees of Medjugorje I have found a chilling divide between their religious profession of dedication to peace and their firm belief in the value of the nuclear deterrent in preserving peace in Europe for 40 years, an inconsistency which often scandalises the atheist and agnostic as well as many Christians,' he wrote in *The Tablet*.[8] This divorce between the values professed in religious belief and their practical application to the concrete issues of today's world underlies fundamentalism. In the Irish context, it can be seen as a desire to return to a triumphalist Catholicism while turning one's back on the urgent challenges of contemporary society.

Ireland is not the only country in which religious fundamentalism has taken on a new lease of life in recent years. The political clout which the religious New Right has in the United States today could not have been foreseen even ten years ago. In that period also, militant Islam has suddenly become a powerful political force on the world stage. And within the Catholic church, what is often termed a Catholic restoration is aggressively in the ascendant.

Common to these phenomena is a reaction against the complexity of modern society and its problems and a hankering for a world of simple certainties. The end result is to ignore very real problems while ascribing responsibility for the problems themselves to those who seek to highlight and address them. In Ireland individuals and groups who oppose any liberalisation of laws relating to sexual matters, or who oppose even discussing these matters, often express such attitudes.

Medjugorje can also give people a cause to which to commit themselves. This in itself can be very positive but when the cause espoused results in a simplistic view of the world and its problems, it can become very dangerous. There may be nothing wrong in itself with telling people to pray to Our Lady in certain ways or to fast once a week as is the advice given at Medjugorje. But where such advice is seen as the way to bring about world peace or social justice then it is simply providing people with a way of avoiding these issues and of neglecting to do something practical about them. It becomes escapist, expressing the sense of paralysis and alienation already described in this chapter.

Social upheaval

Fundamentalism usually raises its head at periods of major social upheaval as long-established social relations, and the values and mores underlying them, begin to break up. This upheaval fosters a deep sense of insecurity among many and they can easily cling to traditional certainties as a way of avoiding the painful process of personal change.

We in Ireland often overlook the extent of social upheaval underway in this country over the past 20 years. Since the 1960s we have emerged swiftly from almost a century and a half of relative cultural stagnation, where the fundamental value system and worldview of most Irish were well defined and predictable. Dissidents were few and had little success in undermining the strong Catholic mono-culture.

While we rightly rejoice that this stagnant and rather sterile culture has finally been challenged and had to give way, we fail to reflect on the implications of these changes. The psychiatrist and author, Anthony Clare, has drawn attention to these:

> Change carries its own problems, and its own advantages. In the Forties and Fifties, Ireland could be said to have been moribund. There were immense problems in the area of mental illness, due to varying factors, such as poorly developed social networks. Now, Ireland is much more alive to the 'disturbances of life'. O'Casey's Dublin had certain securities, but there were also some terrible problems to which they were prone, like alcoholic abuse and violence. In the Eighties, the Irishman is able to be a good deal more candid about many things, but he will be pressurised by the bewildering choices, and the fact that there is no guidance. He is much more like the man everywhere else. But it's all happening fast in Ireland. The changes are occurring more rapidly than they did in Britain, for example. It is all being telescoped. The situation is moving rapidly from one where there were clear guidances and rituals that were accepted by society as worthy of public obeisance, such as Mass, sermons and the notion of a certain collective public acknowledgment of truths and values, to a state where it's all up for grabs. I worry that Ireland won't have enough time to establish for itself an alternative structure.[9]

Many younger Irish people will baulk at the very notion of an 'alternative structure' remembering as they do the domineering hold of Irish Catholicism. Yet Clare draws attention to the need for certain 'guidances and rituals' that can mediate publicly acknowledged truths and values. The swift changes we have encountered have destroyed the traditional ways such truths and values were passed on and reinforced, particularly through the Catholic church.

Today, large sectors of the population fail to encounter in Catholicism any authentic interpretation of their experience and instead discover themselves in the many subcultures around music and drama, alternative politics, Third World solidarity, and the women's movement. In many ways these are the repositories of creativity and new vision for Irish society today. Yet they are having relatively little impact on the wider society, still shaped in its values and outlook by the traditional institutions of church, political parties and media.

As Catholicism retreats from the central place it had in Irish life, the lack of what Clare calls an 'alternative structure' becomes increasingly obvious. In many 'Catholic' countries, socialism provided such an alternative way of embodying a fresh social vision and structures through which to implement that vision in society. In others, entirely new structures have grown up to express the alternative. The most exciting example of this in Western Europe today is West Germany's Green movement. In other parts of the world such as Latin America or the Philippines, this alternative has grown partly within Catholicism and is expressed through a new model of church embodied in structures such as Basic Christian Communities.

What is common to all these examples is the need for new structures to embody an alternative for society. Such structures, be they political parties, grass-roots movements or even communications media, allow those alienated from the traditional structures to participate in the task of fashioning a new society. Furthermore they could challenge a reluctant society to face the malaise and paralysis of the present.

Compared to any Latin American society, Ireland today is characterised by the lack of such alternative structures. The creativity which should be fashioning them remains locked up in subcultures reluctant to make the breakthrough. In the midst of the upheavel of the present, this divorce grows ever more dangerous.

The advent of religious fundamentalism may serve to give a new lease of life and a new confidence to a traditionalist church which has faced the challenge of change in only the

most minimalist of ways. On the political front, the
Progressive Democrats also embody a different kind of
fundamentalism, cloaking in a guise of liberalism what is
fundamentally a dangerous neo-conservatism calculated to
reinforce the dominant elites. Meanwhile, in the absence of
structures embodying a real alternative for the future,
widespread alienation is leading to the growing fragmentation
of Irish society. As the letter on moving statues already quoted
in this chapter said so incisively: 'Breakdown may precede
breakthrough'.

CHAPTER 4

Resources for Change: Education

Commentators and critics often bemoan the conservatism of Irish society. It is not uncommon to hear forcefully expressed the view that we are somehow racially conservative, unable to formulate our own outlook and values, and therefore easily led by a domineering church. Rather than conservatism, however, it may be more accurate to characterise the Irish as complacent and apathetic about the major social problems facing our society, such as economic decline, political violence and social alienation.

Michael Fogarty's major study entitled 'Irish Values and Attitudes', done as part of a European values study and published in 1984, certainly confirmed this picture of a largely conservative and complacent society.[1] In terms of religious, social, moral and political attitudes the Irish are on the conservative end of the European spectrum although the study also showed that this conservative consensus is fast breaking down, particularly among the young.

Faced with what he calls the 'over-comfortable attitudes of the centre and right', Fogarty asks 'whether in today's circumstances the time has not come to sharpen issues and undertake a new campaign of political education. It does not seem to me that present attitudes and levels of activity are such as to bring out political and social issues and promote their solution with the speed and sharpness which the changing circumstances of the country require.'[2]

The sort of political education needed in Ireland is much wider than simply an education in how the political system operates. Such education would do nothing to address the wider issues of complacency and apathy, nor would it mobilise people to become more active in working for political and social change. These are the issues which urgently need to be addressed in any programme of political education in Ireland.

Conscientisation

New methods of education, usually termed 'conscientisation', have had a major impact on the lives of poor people throughout Latin America in recent decades. Such methods involve an entirely new type of education, one that emphasises not only the growth of awareness but also action on that new awareness. It is, as its main proponent, Paulo Freire, insists, an education for liberation and is thus unlike most education which results in domestication or submission to the injustices of the present.

While the term 'conscientisation' is often regarded as very unwieldy when translated into English from the Spanish or Portuguese languages in which it was first developed, it helps draw attention to the two vital elements involved. The first of these is consciousness. Education, in this sense, should be about developing people's awareness of themselves and the world around them, rather than filling them full of facts and information that often have little or no relevance to the situation in which they find themselves. Instead of starting with already defined subjects, therefore, this new form of education seeks to start with the participants' experience and to build on that.

But the second essential element emphasised by the word 'conscientisation' concerns the ability to judge, the ability to act on the new awareness gained. This is the element of 'conscience', the ability to discern and make value judgements on the world around us. One of the great problems of education today is not the lack of awareness of students, rather it is the fact that students have been exposed to so much experience (through television especially) that they are unable to sift it or to appropriate it for themselves. 'Conscientisation' emphasises that people must act on their new-found awareness particularly by involvement in the wider society through action to change it. For this reason, the process of conscientisation is often summed up as a process of 'See-Judge-Act'. As Paulo Freire entitled one of his major books, 'conscientisation' should lead to 'cultural action for freedom'.[3]

This new method of education is now very widespread in that part of the world we know as the Third World. It usually takes place not so much in the formal educational system but rather in informal adult groups. In these, people usually come together out of some social need and there have their eyes opened to the structures of society with particular emphasis on those whom these structures benefit (the privileged) and whom they victimise (the marginalised). The effect on poor people of learning that their marginalisation is not due to some inevitable law of nature but rather is the result of a particular way of organising society is dramatic. It leads them inevitably to become involved in movements for change, whether political groups or social movements.

Throughout Latin America, conscientisation is seen as the educational method best suited to the needs and dignity of the poor. The groups where such education takes place can vary from women's groups to Basic Christian Communities, from TB patients meeting for mutual support to political parties, from neighbourhood assemblies to literacy programmes. But they will always use the people's lived experience as the starting point and always seek to apply their new-found awareness through action for change.

Far more important than adhering to any predetermined method or course outline is this constant reference to the participants' own experience. In this sense, the participants themselves are their own educators; the teacher or group leader is simply someone who helps them to reflect on their experience, to deepen it and then to act on it. Once begun, this process is never-ending since every action attempted itself becomes the source of fruitful discussion and analysis which leads to further action.

Paulo Freire

The Brazilian educationalist, Paulo Freire, first developed these new methods. He says that what is important is not to copy his educational theories but to appropriate his core insight that education must be liberating. 'I sometimes come across a praxis with the name "conscientisation" but which is really very manipulative,' he told me. 'What I'm referring to are very paternalistic types of teaching activity. They might be called "conscientisation" but really they have nothing to do with it. They imply, despite how well-meaning those who use them might be, the preservation of the status quo, divorcing so-called poor people from the process of liberating themselves.'[4]

It was as professor of education in the University of Recife in the impoverished north-east of Brazil in the late 1950s and early 1960s that Paulo Freire first evolved methods of teaching literacy to poor peasants. Instead of coming to the peasants with programmes already worked out, Freire based his methods on what he called 'generative themes' to be discovered in the culture of the learners themselves. These themes, usually key words like 'work' or 'slum', opened up the reality of the learners' lives and thus brought their own experience to the centre of the learning situation.

So successful was Freire in opening poor people's eyes to the injustices which keep them poor that he was arrested and exiled by the Brazilian military when they took power in 1964. He then worked in Chile until 1969 and spent most of the 1970s as a special consultant to the World Council of Churches, based in Geneva. Since 1980, he is back in his native Brazil, where he works with the bishops of the São Paulo archdiocese, the largest in the world.

Instead of trying to copy his methods, what is important, says Freire, is to implement a liberating education. 'In different places and times my methods have been recreated. It is impossible to transplant experience, the experience must be recreated to be authentic. Even the things I did with others in Brazil in the early 1960s cannot be done again in Brazil today. So it is necessary to recreate my ideas according to the historical conditions of those who are trying to recreate me.' As an example, he describes a visit to India where he took part in a seminar with 45 people who worked with peasants and workers. 'They came from different states and the practical condition to participate in the week was not only to have read what I've written but to have worked to put me into practice. When I heard an account of their attempts and struggles I felt for a moment like an Indian!'

Freire is very clear that all education is political. He goes as far as to say that 'we don't have educational problems, we have political problems with educational reflexes'. In saying this he is referring to the over-riding aim of a liberating education which is to make people actors for change in their own societies, to struggle against the injustices which oppress them. In that sense, for Freire, all education is political: it is either designed to bring about political change or, as is the case with so much formal education, it reinforces the status quo.

This understanding has a crucial bearing on the question of whether the formal educational system can ever be an instrument for social change. Freire says this would be a contradiction since, as he puts it, 'the educational system is a sub-system of the wider social system. Then I cannot ask the sub-system to change the global system,' he says.

He illustrates this point by saying that at the time of the French revolution, change didn't come about through the educational system. Rather, he says, the educational system, dominated by the ideas of the previous aristocratic society, finally changed only when the society of which it was a part changed. Similarly today, he added, 'in a society in revolution like Nicaragua, the process of re-inventing a new educational system is very difficult precisely because the old type of education tries to stay in the body of the revolution, representing the opposition to it.'

In our interview, Freire strongly criticised the manipulative teacher and outlined his view that a real teacher must also be constantly learning. 'It is impossible to teach without learning,' he says. 'This doesn't mean that I reject being a teacher. No, I love being a teacher but what I try not to be is a traditional teacher, a dominating teacher, a teacher who has the illusion that he or she knows and that the students come in order to be taught.' But, says Freire, there is another kind of teacher, 'one who is absolutely convinced that it is impossible to teach without learning. For me a revolutionary is a man or a woman who is learning everyday in a permanent process of doing things in order to know. One of the virtues of the revolutionary educator is precisely humility. If we are not humble we cannot be educators, I think.'

During his long years in exile in Europe, Freire experienced the difficulties of implementing a liberating education in our so-called 'developed' societies. 'I learned how difficult it is in the United States or in Europe to invite the students to participate directly in the process of their own education. They really rejected that. It is a question of the ideology of the people, their domination by an ideology of domestication. Both in Geneva and Harvard universities I had the same experience in which the students rejected becoming the subjects of their own education. Of course, I challenged them and finally we got working together.'

Social Analysis
At the heart of the process of conscientisation is what is usually called social analysis. For the process is designed not just to help people understand their own personal or group experience, but to link that to the wider society and even the wider world. Therefore, it is not enough to enable a group of inner-city women, for example, to reflect on their place as marginalised women in the inner-city but also to look at the differences between the inner-city and other city suburbs, and to look at the place of women in the wider society.

Or, to take the crucial issue of work and unemployment, as well as looking at their own immediate experience of being jobless, the unemployed will need to look at issues such as industrial policy, the allocation of resources by government and private business and the role of technology today, all mechanisms generating unemployment. What is crucial in the process of conscientisation is that this happens in a way and at a pace that participants can relate to their own experience and make their own. The more people can be motivated and helped to appropriate their immediate experience, the more will they want to look beyond that to wider aspects.

Through this process, participants are enabled to understand society, to get behind the surface happenings that appear daily in the newspapers or on television and to understand in a deeper way what is really happening. Based on their own experience of poverty and marginalisation, poor people are helped to understand that power and wealth are concentrated in the hands of the few while the majority are excluded. Throughout Latin America simple but well-produced booklets are available as educational aids in this process of opening people's eyes to their reality. Through asking simple but fundamental questions, people are led to a deeper questioning of society and the way it is structured.

How Does Society Function? is one such booklet produced in Lima. It begins by illustrating some of the basic social facts of Latin American life: unemployment, the division between rich and poor, malnourished children, military dictatorships. The booklet then asks: 'Why are things like this? Why does everyone not have work? Why are so many exploited and left without the minimum conditions to live? Why are so many children in this situation? What must be done to improve the conditions of life?' In simple diagramatic form, the booklet then goes on to look at the history of how this situation of inequality has developed. It uncovers the concentration in a few hands of the ownership of industry and land. It examines the ways in which the state serves the interests of the rich and lulls the majority into accepting this situation of injustice through the mass media, the educational system and commercial advertising. Finally, the booklet points to the dependence of Latin America on the United States.

Through my own personal involvement in a family catechesis programme and with a youth group in different Lima shanty towns, I learned to appreciate just how challenging is the process of enabling poor people understand society. In the catechesis group, we opened our weekly meeting with a short 'Hecho de Vida' or Life-Event, based on the everyday experience of the people. This could be an incident such as a family fight, thieves on the local buses, overpricing in the local market or the exploitation of the poor by one of their own. Week after week I was amazed at the way such incidents sparked lively discussion among the participants, a discussion that displayed a keen awareness of local conditions and also an underlying commitment to work for change.

Such a process of education is very different to conventional methods through which I would have told or 'taught' the people the lesson in question. Instead, through their own discussion, they were being enabled to discover it for themselves and in the process grow to appreciate the value of solidarity, of supporting one another and of acting together. Though far slower and more long-term than traditional methods, the results were far deeper and led to genuine transformation not only in the participants but also in the group leader or 'facilitator.'

The surest sign of just how deeply this process changes poor peoples' lives is that participants seek to continue it beyond the immediate need that brought them together. Many of the adults who take part in the family catechetics programme, designed as a course to help them prepare their children for sacraments like First Communion or Confirmation, go on to form Basic Christian Communities through which the same process of awareness-building takes place. These in turn go on to form different types of self-help groups or become active in wider social or political movements for change. Similarly the young people whose meeting I attended each week were themselves planning to produce a small local magazine in order to share their social awareness with a wider public.

Nicaragua

The Nicaraguan literacy campaign is one of the most remarkable examples of a mass programme of conscientisation to have happened anywhere in the world in recent years. For five months from March to August 1980 almost 100,000 Nicaraguan volunteers taught over 400,000 illiterate people to read and write. About half of the volunteers were secondary school students who were organised in brigades and sent to backward rural parts of the country where they lived in the simple huts of the very poor. In urban areas, the teachers were mostly workers and housewives who gave up three hours every evening, five days a week for the five months, going to the homes of illiterates to teach them. At weekends these volunteers had to attend special meetings where their methods were reviewed and their problems discussed.

The campaign was a daunting task for a poor country just recovering from the ravages of the civil war which had finally ousted the dictator Somoza in July 1979. A census taken soon after the Sandinista victory showed that 50.2% of Nicaraguans could not read or write, one of the highest illiteracy rates in Latin America. This immediately became a major priority for the new government, convinced that people needed basic literacy skills before they could become actively involved in the daunting task of transforming their society.

The first step in the campaign was to prepare a basic textbook. Called *The Dawn of the People*, it was based on the ideas of Paulo Freire and on the experiences of the Cuban literacy campaign of 1961. The booklet comprised 23 lessons, all based on the history and tasks of the revolution. Each lesson had an accompanying photograph to initiate discussion and the lesson had a key sentence summing up the theme of the photograph.

For example, the first lesson shows a well-known photo of Cesar Augusto Sandino, the hero of the Sandinista revolution. The key sentence reads: 'Sandino, guia de la revolución'

(Sandino, guide of the revolution). The words 'la revolución' are then used to teach the five vowels, a e i o u. The method is built up through lessons on such themes as 'The popular masses made the insurrection', 'To spend little, to save resources and to produce much is to make the revolution', 'Woman has always been exploited, the revolution makes possible her liberation.'

Through the process of teaching people to read and write, therefore, their eyes were also opened to the history of exploitation in Nicaragua and to the possibilities created by the revolution. This aspect of the campaign was dismissed by some outside critics as political indoctrination. Visiting classes in progress and speaking to those learning to read and write, however, I was struck by just how meaningful the content of the lessons was to them. For they were also beginning to understand Nicaraguan society and get a sense of their own power. To have designed a literacy campaign around relatively meaningless themes of everyday life such as shopping or a day's outing, as would be done in the West, would have been very patronising to the participants.

One evening late in the campaign, I visited a small class of four people in the living room of a house in one of Managua's poor suburbs or *barrios*. Here the teacher, a TV and radio mechanic, was dictating a sentence from lesson 22. 'The true church,' he read, 'should not be negligent of the needs of the people.' His students, one a 69 year old man and the other a 49 year old woman, slowly wrote it down and showed it around proudly. The other two students, two women, one 42 years old and the other 58 years old, sat on the beds in the other half of the room; they had already finished the course. One of them showed me a simple letter she had written thanking the government for the campaign; this had been published in the daily newspaper *Barricada*. Overall that *barrio* had just under 1,000 illiterates and 235 teachers. Their success rate in the first five months was over 80%.

My visit to the rural community of El Tular showed the other face of the campaign. Here 26 students from the Marist

College in the nearby town of Estelí were teaching half the population of this scattered mountainous community – some 100 people. For the five months of the campaign, they shared the lot of the local people, sleeping on the dirt floors of their simple huts, eating their often unhygienic food and sharing their daily tasks. Then every evening, with the help of oil lamps provided by a Swedish trade union, the whole family gathered around the table to learn to read and write.

Overseeing the process were four teachers from the town and two students of journalism from the University of Managua. These latter were directing another aspect of the campaign in El Tular as the members of the 'literacy brigade' there were also collecting accounts from the people of the fighting in the area during the civil war. All these accounts, together with poetry written by the newly literate, were to be published by the Ministry of Culture.

Back in Managua, the campaign was officially brought to an end on 23 August 1980, at a mass rally attended by over 350,000 people. 'After five months of hard struggle in the countryside, in the mountains and in the towns, we have managed to teach to read and to write 406,056 Nicaraguans, reducing the illiteracy rate from 50.35% to 12.96% of the population over 10 years of age,' said the campaign director, Fr Fernando Cardenal SJ, addressing the crowd. As he spoke, a large red and black flag bearing the words 'Nicaragua, territory victorious over illiteracy' was raised and a flame mounted on top of a giant cluster of poles shaped as pencils was lit.

As well as teaching poor people to read and write, the literacy campaign was an intensely educational experience for those who taught them. For many who came from middle class or rich backgrounds, it offered a first-hand experience of how the majority of Nicaraguans live and helped break down the division between urban and rural which can be the source of so much misunderstanding. Through their five months spent with poor peasants, many of the secondary school students found their values changed and their commitment to building a new Nicaragua strengthened. Meanwhile, the process of adult education continued under a Vice-Ministry of Adult Education set up as the campaign ended.

Ireland

The educational theories of Paulo Freire have also had a major impact in parts of the developed world. He told me how he thought they could be applied in Ireland:

> I think it is possible to work with some of my ideas in Ireland. I am sure it is. The question is how to use the historical limits that you have and also the question is to re-create, to adapt.
>
> It is a question of knowing – how to challenge the oppressed people of Ireland to know, to read their reality? To do this in São Paulo I have to do it one way; for you to do it may mean that you have to do something completely different. But the objective is to be involved in a process of knowing. I absolutely agree that it is harder for people in Europe to realise that they are oppressed because the levels of alienation are much more strong that ours here [in Brazil]. Why? Because the contradictions are much less visible.

Freire's description of the task to be undertaken involves two elements: firstly, to enable the oppressed and marginalised to discover the nature of their marginalisation and its causes and, secondly, to do that through their active involvement in action to overcome this marginalisation. Central to applying such methods of education here in Ireland would be a social analysis through which people can be helped to demystify the structures of society and to uncover the real structures of power.

These methods would enable people, particularly those who most suffer from the way our society is presently structured, to uncover the nature of Irish society far more effectively than any lectures could do. They would quickly begin to see that real power is held not so much by our elected representatives but by the leaders of big business, large farmers and the bankers who mould government policies to suit their interests, policies which marginalise increasingly large sectors of the population. They would quickly see also how the major social institutions legitimise this structure of power – the educational system, the law, the media, the churches. This is the way the oppressed experience society.

The importance of this process for the future direction of Irish society was highlighted by Fr Donal Dorr when writing about the way 'in which the choices of the Irish people need to be widened. It is a matter of *who* makes the key decisions about our future. At present they are made by a small number of senior civil servants, who give advice to the politicians, by the directors of the banks and of multinational companies, and by the policy-makers of the Church. Those who are looking for significant changes in Irish society can easily be tempted to spend their time and energy in trying to influence this elite group of decision-makers. But the most important change that needs to be made is to enable the powerless and even the alienated to participate in shaping our society.'[5]

What is striking here in Ireland is the absence of materials to enable this process of education, or conscientisation as it is often called in Third World countries, to take place. Much of what is available comes from church sources which makes it suspect in the eyes of some groups. Yet books such as *Social Analysis in the Light of the Gospel* and *Ireland Today* by Fr Sean Healy SMA and Sr Brigid Reynolds SM of the Conference of Major Religious Superiors (CMRS)[6] and *Unemployment: Crisis or Opportunity?* by Fr John Sweeney SJ of the Centre for Faith and Justice[7] are filling a very major gap. By contrast, the research and analysis published by research centres, universities or political parties is beyond the reach of many people. The publications of the Workers Party are perhaps the only exception. A lot more needs urgently to be done in popularising the kind of research being sponsored by groups like the Economic and Social Research Institute (ESRI) and the Institute for Public Administration (IPA), and in developing new methods of popular education capable of helping Irish people read their own reality.

CHAPTER 5

Resources for Change: Media

For Ireland, as for so many of the world's countries, the coming of television has led to a revolution in communication. Its influence in breaking down the narrow parochialism and insularity of Irish life is often referred to. The media, and particularly television, constitute today perhaps the greatest single influence in moulding popular views of the world, superseding school and church as society's main socialising agents.

But for all our exposure to media, we are remarkably uncritical of its influence. True, people will grumble about this programme or that, but such grumbling usually remains confined to individual items or series. Few media watchers, listeners or readers have any sense of the narrow consensus about society being constantly communicated to them, a consensus that mirrors the interests of those who control our society.

This narrow consensus is a further factor reinforcing the sense of passivity and complacency widespread in Ireland today. As the famous MacBride report on world communications, published in 1980, pointed out 'Communication can be an instrument of power, a revolutionary weapon, a commercial product, or a means of education; it can serve the ends of either liberation or oppression, of either the growth of the individual personality or the drilling of human beings into uniformity.'[1] While some of these labels may describe elements of the Irish media, none of them are adequate to describe it fully. But they do serve to remind us that the media are never neutral in society; they play a definite social and political role which needs to be more fully examined.

Ireland falls down badly in this respect as compared to Latin American countries. There, even with overt censorship and repressive governments, one encounters a flourishing opposition media reflecting not just middle class interests but also those of the dispossessed masses. These media provide a voice for the criticisms, concerns and activities of those sectors of society marginalised and excluded from power and its benefits. Aware that the mainstream media reflect the views and concerns of the rich and powerful, these alternative media, as they are often called, challenge this narrow consensus and show that it does not reflect the experience of large sectors of society.

The media: alienating images

Underlying this alternative media is a widespread awareness of the role of the mass media in society today. As a conference in São Paulo, Brazil, on the church and the new communication order, held in October 1982, concluded:

> The mass media are not utilised for the common good. They are in the hands of business corporations and they are thus controlled by a small minority of the population. Instead of being used for the benefit of all society, they disseminate material designed to reinforce established values and neutralise the people's desire for change. The flow of information is directly controlled by a handful of international power centres, ruling out the possibility for all to make their voices heard.[2]

This control of information by small elites is easily demonstrated. Five international news agencies control 80% of the world-wide news flow. These are the two US agencies, United Press International (UPI) and Associated Press (AP), Agence France Presse of France (AFP), the British Reuters and the Soviet agency, Tass. Two-thirds of foreign news in Latin American daily newspapers comes from the two US agencies. Three broadcasting networks in the First World provide all the international news footage every day for Third World TV stations. In Jamaica, for example, not only is all international news taken directly from US networks, but the very news programme itself is simply a US programme re-broadcast by the Jamaican Broadcasting Corporation. This is common throughout Latin America. Over half the films shown in Latin America come from Hollywood and two-thirds of all advertising in Latin America is controlled by US-based firms.

Such control, mirroring the economic dominance of the world by these same countries, is justified by the facile slogan 'Freedom of the Press'. Behind such freedom lies a vested interest in controlling the world-wide flow of information so as to ensure it does not challenge the economic dominance of the world's powerful countries. Thus the dominant media constantly select and order 'news' in such as way as to reinforce the position of the great powers. What the United States or the EEC does is seen as reasonable and normative while the actions of other countries, particularly when they deviate from these 'norms', are subtly undermined and labelled as 'extremist', 'radical' or just downright 'dangerous'.

Information, or as the media usually calls it, news, is never objective. Recent studies have identified the main criteria governing what is considered 'newsworthy' in the West's media. For facts or events to become 'news', they must concern elite nations or elite people, be couched in personal rather than structural terms and be negative rather than positive. Reflecting these criteria is the fact that in the United States more journalists cover happenings in the White House than cover the whole of the rest of the world. For their editors, the slightest utterance of the US president is more important than the great struggles and sufferings of the world's poor.

A simple example illustrates this and applies it to the Irish media. In the midst of the crucial and highly significant nationalisation of the Peruvian banking system by President Alan Garcia from July to October 1987, RTÉ carried an item from Peru on their 8.00am news one morning. This concerned an invasion by bats of a village in the Andes mountains. Perhaps, it was intended as a 'light' item, to give a little colour to the otherwise heavy news bulletin. Yet at no time during the long months that the bank nationalisation was being

discussed in Congress or being implemented, did any organ
of the Irish news media report in any substance on what was
taking place. It goes without saying that the nationalisation,
an effort by the government to wrest economic control of
credit from the elites for the benefit of the poor majority, is
a significant struggle from which we could all learn. Instead
there was an effective media blackout on that and we were
treated to the trivial.

We hear a lot about the marriages, divorces, births and
deaths of the rich in the developed world, while we hear
almost nothing except disasters, earthquakes, coups and
famines about the rest of the world. As media specialist Johan
Galtung said in a recent paper:

> It is very important to note that such tragedies are taken out of
> their structural context – a context partly created and perpetuated
> by forces in the industrialised world in general and the First
> World in particular. This type of reporting mainly serves to keep
> persons in centre [rich] countries convinced of the miserable
> living conditions in periphery countries, and consequently of how
> fortunate they are not to be there.[3]

Reporting is constantly coloured by personal prejudices and
perspectives. Editing involves constant choice. Out of such
reporting and choices, usually made on our behalf by people
we never hear of, comes the information and the news that
fashions our view of the world around us. The very structure
of the large news agencies shows where such filtering takes
place. A good news agency reporter in San Salvador or
Managua may be reporting the struggles of those countries as
sensitively as possible and from the perspective of the poor
majorities, yet his or her story has first to go to New York,
Paris or London where it is edited by someone who has
probably never been to the country in question. The version
of the reporter's story which is finally received in newsrooms
around the world, however, is the editor's rather than the
reporter's version.

More often, the reporters themselves, nationals of North
America or Western Europe, are little attuned to the real

dynamic or context of events they are covering and respond much more to the needs of their editors rather than working from any serious understanding of the society they are covering. For example, a survey was done in Brazil in the three months of August, September and October 1984 at the height of the Vatican's scrutiny of the liberation theologian, Fr Leonardo Boff. This examined all foreign news agency reports on the case during this period and found that 88.3% were clearly hostile to liberation theology, completely distorting the widespread popular support for the theologian in Brazil at the time.[4]

Living in the Third World, one regularly encounters how ridiculous this system can become. For example, many Lima newspapers, with few staff and run on a small budget, depend on the large news agencies not just for their foreign news but even for national stories. Therefore, it was not uncommon to find stories appearing in Lima papers about events in the city which had first been edited in New York or London. Imagine a US or British editor editing a story on Ireland for publication in a Dublin paper!

We may think we are learning about the world around us, but more often than not what we are really learning about when we read our papers or when we watch our TV news is how the world is viewed from New York, London or Paris. It is therefore little wonder that most see the majority of the world's peoples as little capable of running their own affairs while never questioning the right of the few powerful countries to dominate and control the world for their own enrichment. The Reagan administration's treatment of Nicaragua is but the most scandalous example of the way the world's powerful treat the rest. It indicates the continuing legacy of colonialism.

A New World Information and Communication Order

While one encounters little or no concern for this cultural colonialism here in Ireland, it is a very live issue indeed in

Latin America and other parts of the Third World. For this reason UNESCO set up a commission under the chairmanship of Seán MacBride in 1976 to examine the world's communication order. Its report, adopted by UNESCO in 1980, has given impulse to the struggle for what is now officially defined as a New World Information and Communication Order (NWICO). It has also made the name of Seán MacBride a household name throughout the Third World since the report is always referred to as the MacBride Report and the issue itself is intimately linked with his name.

The official name of the report, *Many Voices, One World*, indicates its main thrust. Seeing a more free and balanced flow of information among the world's peoples as an essential element of the struggle for a more peaceful and just world, the report urges a greater democratisation of communication both among countries and among different social sectors within each country. Its detailed recommendations cover such diverse areas as:

- ensuring an adequate sharing of new technological developments among the countries of the world,
- creating mechanisms whereby the general public can play a more active role both in communication itself and in the management of the media,
- raising the professional standards of journalists and media managers,
- reassessing conventional standards of news selection and reporting,
- establishing policies to foster cultural identity and creativity,
- introducing measures to ensure greater equality and co-operation among all the world's peoples in use of the media.

One paragraph gives the flavour of the report's content:

Diversity and choice in the content of communication are a precondition for democratic participation. Every individual and particular groups should be able to form judgements on the basis of a full range of information and a variety of messages and opinions and have the opportunity to share these ideas with others. The development of decentralised and diversified media should provide larger opportunities for a real, direct involvement of the people in communication processes.[5]

Despite the report's very moderate content and tone, however, it was received with fury by the governments and news agencies of the West. Discarding even the mildest semblance of 'objectivity' in their coverage of the issue, the news agencies immediately labelled the MacBride Report as a totalitarian plot to hand control of the media over to governments. UNESCO's subsequent attempts to implement the report led to the withdrawal of the United States from the organisation and the threat by Britain to do so. The inability of the Western media even to consider the report's analyses and recommendations is itself an indication of just how successful the MacBride commission was in uncovering where the true control of the world's media lies.

The Media in Ireland

The MacBride Report offers us some guidelines with which to examine the media in Ireland. Before examining the content of the media, these lead us to look firstly at who controls it. This control tends to determine much more the social role it plays than do the presence of some excellent and very committed journalists in both print and broadcasting media. In radio and television the question of control is easily answered – the government through the RTÉ authority. This is about to change, however, as commercial interests will largely control the new local broadcasting network to be set up. The newspapers already display this commercial control, with two groups, the Independent and Press, having well over half the market in the Republic. By international standards this is considered a very high concentration of ownership. What is interesting about these two groups is their traditional political affiliations, the Press being closely linked to Fianna Fáil, and the Independent Group (which now also controls *The Sunday World*) having rather looser links to Fine Gael. More significant about the latter, however, is the control exercised by Tony O'Reilly. As *Irish Times* editor Conor Brady has written of the directors chosen by O'Reilly, 'they represent broadly, a cross-section of the successful, free-enterprise business people of contemporary Ireland.'[6] What Brady fails to mention is that they also, through O'Reilly, represent some interests of multinational capital in Ireland. The remaining two national papers, *The Irish Times* and *The Sunday Tribune*, are more formally independent but they cater for a similar readership of the urbanised, middle and upper middle classes. Outside Dublin, *The Cork Examiner* is the most important paper, aspiring to be a national daily but having a concentration of its market in the Munster area. It is owned by the Crosbie family which has close Fine Gael links. The final factor to be pointed out about the national press is the absence of foreign ownership, a factor increasingly important in major British dailies. Tony O'Reilly's influence in the Independent Group as well as the high circulation of British papers here, however, lessen the significance of this factor.

A similar narrow structure of control can be identified in the provincial press. Here again, the Independent Group has the largest single share with 13% of the market. The remainder is shared between some forty small locally-owned newspapers most of which, however, have a near monopoly of the market in their own areas. As described by John Horgan, journalism lecturer in Dublin's NIHE, these newspapers' owners and usually their editors 'form part of a local power structure that can involve, for example, the local professional stratum (auctioneers, doctors, lawyers), the local bureaucracy (health boards and local authority officials) and the local political presence (councillors, TDs, etc)'.[7] It is the interests of this group in the local community that are served by these newspapers which, says Horgan, tend to reinforce 'the dominant conservative values within the community.'

With control of the media in the hands of such a narrow group there is little need for the kind of overt censorship one encounters in many countries where sectors of the media reflect the interests of oppressed sectors of the population. That is not to say, however, that overt censorship is not exercised in the Irish media, particularly the use of Section

31 against a legal political party, Sinn Féin. But, as John Horgan has pointed out, controversy over Section 31 has 'obscured the history of a long and quite overt tradition of government intervention in the affairs of the privately-owned print media'. He concludes that this is less necessary today because of a 'semi-equilibrium' between journalists and those on whom they report 'that is rarely disturbed'.[8]

There are many areas in which this semi-equilibrium can be readily identified. The media concentrate on the elites, giving the impression that their interests are those of all of us. This is reinforced through chat shows, through soap operas, through advertising and even through current affairs coverage. Despite their obsession with the rich and successful, however, the media fail to examine in any thorough way their financial and business interests and acquiesce in these as much as they expose them. For example, the growing concentration of ownership, especially of companies and brand names that are familiar names in every household in Ireland, is almost never exposed by the media.

Instead we are regularly treated to scares about high levels of crime or social welfare spongers. These are rarely substantiated by any examination of the evidence yet they constantly recur. Where the rich are criticised it is always as individuals rather than as a class; where the poor are criticised, all are implicated.

Examination of key policy decisions, particularly in economic and social affairs, accepts the basic agenda set down by the establishment and rarely promotes any critical examination of that agenda. Examples of this can be seen in the way the health cuts and the debt crisis are covered.

While sectors of the media may be critical about aspects of these cuts, the media as a whole have accepted the establishment's unsubstantiated contention that this 'harsh medicine' must be accepted as the only way to bring the debt under control. Indeed Charles Haughey, from being the *bête noire* of much of the print media, has overnight become its darling because of his sudden conversion to austerity.

Furthermore, we hear virtually nothing about how other large debtors are coping with their problems, the alternative solutions being proposed by them, or the growing criticisms of the international economic order emerging from their debt discussions. Because we fail to examine the issue, we feel trapped by the narrow orthodoxy of the 'experts'.

Coverage of disadvantaged and marginalised groups is usually patronising and almost never allows their social critique to be communicated. Labour party TD, Michael D. Higgins' account of his experience with the media expresses that of anybody who espouses a critical alternative:

> Minority political viewpoints find themselves being treated, at best, paternalistically and more usually in a dismissive way. There are some minority voices, of course, that cannot be present at all. My experience over ten years living as a socialist in the periphery is one of being presented as a political deviant.[9]

As a result, our view of society and the wider world is extremely narrow, permitting nothing of the diversity of communication called for by the MacBride report and reinforcing all the time a narrow and largely unexamined consensus about the future direction of Irish society. Few would find their experience of society incisively interpreted by the Irish media. It must be concluded that much of the Irish media serves as an instrument of power and as a commercial product, reinforcing the status quo rather than challenging it in any thorough way.

Alternative media

One of the more compelling aspects of the MacBride Report is its strong emphasis that communication is a right for all. It is something we easily forget, accustomed as we are to seeing our airwaves and our print media dominated by the elites. In Latin America, however, through the growth of popular forms of communication, the poor and marginalised are finding the media to communicate their own experience and concerns. We in Ireland have a lot to learn from them.

Ms Regina Festa is a Brazilian journalist who spent 14 years working firstly as a journalist on São Paulo's leading newspaper *Folha de São Paulo* and later as director of 13 monthly magazines. In 1978, however, she moved to the poor suburb of São Miguel Paulista to work in more popular media of communication. Together with groups of local people, she helped establish the Centre of Communication and Popular Education of São Miguel. Though she has given a lot of her time to the centre, she emphasises that she is not the director. 'Mine is always the work of giving support to the people themselves, never telling them what to do,' she says.

The variety of forms of communication developed by the centre witness to the creativity of these people. They produce a monthly newspaper, *Grita Povo,* reporting on local issues such as strikes, the problems of housing, the poor state of public transport, informing on church activities and educating the people on important issues such as Brazil's foreign debt problem or national politics. The centre has a video team, which produces material to 'pose questions and animate discussions on issues of local importance,' as Ms Festa describes it. This team also documents the processions and *fiestas*, the strikes and struggles of the people. Another team is made up exclusively of children between the ages of three and eight who produce their own puppet shows for other young children. 'We want to respect their infant world,' says Ms Festa.

The rich culture of the local people, many of whom have migrated from the north-east of Brazil with its own very distinctive culture, is collected by another group at the centre. They tape the people telling the stories of their past and collect their very distinctive *cordeles* – pictures printed from handmade wood carvings, with long poems inside describing the lives of those who made them.

The centre has its own bookshop selling the simple booklets produced throughout Brazil for conscientising the people. Furthermore the centre produces its own simple booklets on such topics as how to organise a meeting or to build up a community. Other items on sale in the bookshop include posters and T-shirts produced in the centre using a silk screen process. Situated in the centre of São Miguel, the centre is a lively place constantly used by people. On weekends it comes alive with the sounds of groups learning to play the guitar and on Saturday evenings it is used to show Brazilian and other Latin American films which would never be shown in the commercial cinemas.

Ms Festa says she finds a great tension between what she learned in her training and her present practice of journalism:

> We learned a North American journalism, with its myth of objectivity and its very fixed methods of working. But among the people of the shanty towns I have found a great school of journalism. It was a very interesting experience in my professional life because among them I found I was treated as an equal, and they told me what to do just as they told each other. You need to discover much humility, because it is not a question of 'what I can do' but what the community I am part of decides to do. I must be at the service of this process; my intellectual capabilities must be an instrument of this people.

Reflecting on her life in mainstream journalism, Ms Festa says that she used 'to live and work in a minority world'. Instead, the people with whom she now works constitute a majority. Throughout Brazil centres are springing up to help give a voice to that majority. At national meetings they have held over 100 centres have been represented, 90% of them of christian inspiration, says Ms Festa. With the centre now thriving, she wants to move on to new tasks. Among these is a plan to develop non-written forms of communication through which workers' and peasants' groups can communicate with each other.

CHAPTER 6

Resources for Change: People's Power

When referring to the impact of government spending cuts on the poor or to the growing masses of marginalised people in societies throughout the world, commentators often make a fundamental mistake. They assume that people can only suffer so much, that eventually a point is reached when they will rebel against those whom they see as responsible for their suffering. While examples of such spontaneous rebelliousness can be seen in history, far more common and remarkable is the submissiveness of the poor to their lot. In fact, it often appears the case that the poorer people get, the less likely they are to protest or even criticise since all their energies are channelled into the simple task of survival. It is not accidental that most revolutions in history have been led by the middle classes.

Yet, one of the things that most distinguishes today's world is the growing emergence of the poor masses on to the stage of history. In countries as different as Iran, Nicaragua, South Africa and the Philippines, the revolt of significant sectors of the population against tryannical rulers has shown its potential for change. The world's media coined the term 'people power' to explain the stirring scenes in the centre of the Philippine capital, Manila, in February 1986 when masses of ordinary people blocked the tanks of the dictator, Ferdinand Marcos.

Communicated daily on television screens around the world, these scenes seemed to symbolise the potential of mass, peaceful revolt. Paradoxically, however, as commentators have subsequently shown, that was much more a middle class revolt leading to no substantial change in the structure of power in the Philippines. The people's real challenge to the entrenched oligarchy is yet to come and will involve a far more difficult transition than did the accession of Cory Aquino.

The changes wrought by 'People's Power' in Nicaragua and Iran over recent years have been more far-reaching, leading to fundamental changes in both societies. The greatest test of this is the widespread support still enjoyed by their new governments despite the hardships of war in both cases. No matter how much we may be appalled by the religious fundamentalism and the clericalism of the Iranian revolution, what cannot be denied is that it is the fruit of a massive popular revolt against a tyrant who was staunchly supported by the West.

In countries such as South Africa and El Salvador, the determined resistance of the ruling elites and their foreign backers to any change has been unable to break the back of an aware and mobilised public. Far-reaching changes are on the way in both countries; they may be delayed but they cannot be avoided.

Underlying this phenomenon is a new understanding of politics. This entails a process of empowering people, particularly the poor and marginalised, to find their own voice and become a power in their own right. As the leading Peruvian intellectual, Fr Gustavo Gutierrez, has written, the present-day reality of Latin America is marked by 'the clear awareness that something new [is] afoot, something no repression could ever again quell or crush: a people's will to self-affirmation and to life'. And, quoting the great Peruvian socialist thinker, José Carlos Mariátegui, who said that 'pessimism comes from reality, optimism comes from action,' Gutierrez urges that 'what is sorely needed here is not a condemnation of reality, but a conviction that that reality can and must be transformed by the action of the people.'[1]

In many parts of Latin America today, this action of the people is expressed through a myriad of small, local groups through which slum-dwellers, small street traders, trade unionists, women, young people, christians, and others, come together to reflect on their situation and take action to change it. Such action may take the form of organising street protests, establishing co-operatives, setting up support groups for refugees, publicising human rights abuses by the security forces, or founding *comedores* through which a group of local women pool their meagre resources to cook one hot meal a day. Through involvement in such groups, the people develop their political awareness and discover their own power. This growing organisation of the poor and marginalised, from grass-roots up, is usually called the *movimiento popular*, the people's movement.

Peru: The People's Movement

Villa El Salvador is not only the largest shanty town in Peru with over 300,000 inhabitants, but also one of the largest in Latin America. Founded on 11 May 1971, it stands today as a living witness to what organised groups of ordinary people can achieve. Few peoples have faced such inhospitable surroundings from which to construct an urban centre. Situated on the outskirts of Lima, some 35 kilometres from the city centre, it is bounded by the foothills of the Andes to the east and the endless Pacific ocean to the west. Here the desert plain is so dry that no plant grows naturally. Even today as one looks out over the town from the paved road which by-passes it on the east, it is the vast expanse of dry, fine sand which dominates the view. Despite its size, Villa El Salvador still seems from a distance to be fighting the elements in order to establish its right to occupy this plain at all.

It is not money that has transformed the desert into a living urban centre. Only in 1987 did the town for the first time get a grant from the Peruvian government. Neither have private developers or investors shown any interest; those who seek financial profit are hardly attracted by a desert full of poor people. As one young inhabitant who grew up in Villa remembers:

The cold and the gloom, the heat and the dust, were the constant companions of the inhabitants. There were no paved roads, no schools, no health clinics, no water or light. . . there was only a desert. At first all one could see were thousands of *estera* huts [made from reed matting]; little by little through organisation, through voluntary, communal work and through the people's determination, our town was built.

What the progressive Peruvian government of General Juan Velasco Alvarado gave Villa El Salvador was the right to be self-governing. It has proved its greatest and most enduring legacy, far more important than if the people had received large grants of money. For, from the beginning, the people constituted themselves into what must be one of the most democratic societies anywhere in the world. This is organised on the basis of each block, constituting 24 houses. These families meet regularly to discuss their problems and elect four leaders. Their responsibilities include education about hygiene and preventative health, ensuring the people get their fair share of any services available such as light and water, overseeing the opening of little shops for the people and, generally, taking note of any particular hardships the block may have.

Each group of 16 blocks is called a 'residential group'. Once a year the inhabitants of each residential group come together in a general assembly and elect a group of eight leaders to a central committee. The final stage in this democratic organisation is called the Communal Executive Council, elected at a convention every two years. Made up of eleven members, this has final responsibility for the people's welfare in all the 110 residential groups which make up the town today.

Because of this structure, functioning successfully since 1973, Villa El Salvador is officially known as a 'self-managing city'; the acronym of the letters of this name in Spanish spell CUAVES, the title of their unique democracy. This structure, which has grown up in response to the people's needs, functions adequately only because tens of thousands of people are willing to give freely of their time and energy in the service of one another. Its uniqueness was recognised in 1986 when it was nominated for the Nobel Peace Prize and in 1987 it won the prestigious Principe de Asturias prize, awarded by the Spanish royal family.

The achievements of Villa's inhabitants are remarkable. People will freely remind the visitor of the days when they had to walk a few kilometres to a bus route or to the nearest water pump. Now a number of bus routes link Villa El Salvador to the centre of Lima while water is piped to most homes. The date when the first electricity was switched on, 24 December 1975, is still remembered, another achievement gained by putting pressure on the public authorities through mass marches into the city centre.

It is a matter of great pride that 80% of homes now have electricity and 75% have running water and sewerage. The area is, however, still subject to frequent blackouts and most homes have water only two or three hours every second day. While most streets remain unpaved, two main roads have been tarred and many enterprising blocks have carefully built concrete footpaths through the sand.

Apart from these essential services, 34 schools have been built under a system whereby the parents themselves do the building, working at weekends or in the evening. As a result the literacy rate is 97%, perhaps the most remarkable achievement of all. This is 11% above the national average for Peru which itself is much higher than that in most of its neighbouring countries. Built also have been public meeting places in each one of the 110 residential groups, health centres and sports complexes.

While these are being built through the voluntary effort of the local people, almost no one in the whole town has yet finished building their own homes. As is the case throughout the shanty towns of Lima, building a home is a life-long task. A new room, a roof, a window or a door is added as family savings allow. The most visible sign of an economic recession is the lack of building activity and the piles of bricks neatly stacked on a roof or in a yard, awaiting better times until there is enough money to use them.

If the CUAVES acts as a framework through which people's energies are channelled, numerous other self-help organisations have grown up in response to particular needs. Foremost among these are women's groups, grouped now into a Women's Popular Federation for Villa El Salvador and comprising up to a hundred different organisations. Women come together in Mothers' Clubs to discuss their problems, in knitting co-operatives to gain some meagre income from knitting goods for sale, in school milk programmes through which they organise the distribution of a glass of milk to each school child every day, and in communal kitchens.

Through the growth of these organisations can also be charted the growing poverty of the people. This is particularly true of the food kitchens which experienced a marked growth in the mid-1980s as the Peruvian economy was going through a severe crisis due, partly, to the imposition of right-wing monetarist policies. Though some receive food from voluntary organisations, most are formed by groups of women who buy and cook food communally. This not only reduces costs but frees the women from the daily task of cooking for their families, increasing their chances of finding some work. Women have also come together in committees to plant trees around the area, an essential activity to add colour to the drabness of the desert. Already half a million trees have been planted and each one has to be carefully nurtured and watered if it is not to die, a symbol of the people's daily dedication to building a better future for all.

Ireland: Political Illiteracy

In Ireland, this level of popular involvement in political life and action is almost entirely missing. For example, Michael Fogarty, in his study of Irish values and attitudes, found a very low level of interest in politics. Altogether only 5% admitted to being active in politics while 44% expressed complete disinterest. Alongside this lack of political involvement, Fogarty found a high involvement in voluntary religious, welfare and youth organisations. Yet, unlike in Latin America where such involvement might quickly politicise people, here in Ireland it is often seen as a substitute for politics.

What Fogarty uncovers, therefore, can be called a high level of political illiteracy. People see politics as a means of gaining favours (or even their due) from the state rather than as a way of changing society. The voters relate to individual issues which affect them rather than to differing visions of society. Ideologues of the right are considered as much an anomaly as are those of the left. This political illiteracy is quite deliberately maintained by most Irish politicians and the system they perpetuate.

Irish politicians deal with grievances not as political issues but as individual problems. The careers of most TDs are built not on their contribution to political decision-making about the great issues facing our society, but rather on their ability to deliver to their constituents everything from telephone boxes to jobs in the civil service. The lack of concern about issues and policies means that dramatic about-turns can be done by Fianna Fáil overnight without it causing any great concern to most TDs or party supporters. As a result our political life is dominated by pragmatic and short-term responses to problems as they arise. There is little or no ideological debate in which differing options for the future can be presented and developed.

Apart from the small number of serious left-wing politicians, few politicians are burdened by strong convictions. Those they hold relate to traditional nationalist issues around which Irish politics defined itself in the formative years of the last century and first two decades of this one. Strong convictions about issues such as poverty, unemployment and injustice are rare in Irish political life and are more an electoral liability than an asset.

This was indicated clearly at the end of 1987 in the almost unprecedented Fianna Fáil backbench revolt on extradition, a revolt that forced Charles Haughey to introduce a series of safeguards for those to be extradited, in the face of strong

British opposition. This revolt stemmed from the nationalist convictions which still live on within the Fianna Fáil party. No such convictions have surfaced, however, against the health and education cuts. Any murmurings from the backbenches on these have been motivated more by a fear of personal political damage than by any deeply held conviction that such cuts are damaging in themselves. As a result Mr Haughey has had little difficulty ensuring party support for them or of maintaining his party's lead in the opinion polls.

The observation is often made that the relationship between TDs and their constituents is clientalist in nature, fostering a sense of individual dependence and reducing politics to solving individual problems. The obverse side of this coin is rarely looked at, however. If most TDs take little interest in politics or policy outside the narrow confines of their own constituency, then who makes, scrutinises and changes policy? The political vacuum left by the clientalist TD has been filled by different interest groups, representing, among others, industry, finance, farmers, the trade unions, educationalists and the churches. They keep a careful watch on political decisions affecting their institutional interests and know how to apply pressure to ensure decisions in their favour.

It is the poor and marginalised who suffer as a result. As the least organised in society, they have no voice and no strong organisations through which their interests and concerns can be articulated. Indeed, society does not even acknowledge them as sectors to be taken into account. This is clearly shown at budget time every year when representatives of industry and finance, of farmers' organisations and the trade unions, are invited to react on radio and television. Yet the unemployed, the Travellers, those on social welfare, the homeless, are never given a voice; they are considered as groups whose interests society can ignore.

Much key policy-making, therefore, takes place in secrecy rather than in the open light of public debate and involves trade offs between well-organised sectors of the population. Dr Noel Browne is one of the few Irish politicians who tried to resist this behind-the-scenes politiking when he revealed publicly the hierarchy's pressures to change his Mother and Child Bill. Such a fundamental act of democratic accountability deeply shocked his colleagues in government and ensured he would never again become a minister. Such a system makes it next to impossible for government and politicians to develop coherent plans for the future and to implement these even when they interfere with sectional interests.

Rather than a staunch ideological conservatism, what emerges from even a cursory examination of the Irish political system is a picture of political life and institutions marginalised from the real concerns of people. Credibility in the institutions of Irish life (politics, business, the Church, trade unions, the media, the educational system) is low and falling, according to Michael Fogarty, in his study. Alienation he found to be particularly high among marginalised groups like the unemployed. Alongside this Fogarty found a demand for active participation in decision-making both in industry and in politics.

While these latter findings would correlate with what one finds throughout Latin America, the big difference is that in Ireland the demand for participation in society is not giving rise to new movements through which it could be exercised. This is particularly true in the case of the poor and marginalised. Ireland still awaits its *movimiento popular*.

Rather than representing the interests of the people, particularly those fundamentally conflicting interests of the powerful and powerless, the Irish political system has, therefore, developed elaborate mechanisms to prevent the emergence of the marginalised and deprived on to the political stage. What Bishop Pedro Casaldáliga said in a recent interview about Brazilian democracy could equally well be applied to Ireland: 'In the type of system we live in democracy is relative.'

Populism

Fianna Fáil has no monoply on clientalism or basic political pragmatism; Fine Gael and Labour have also been able practitioners. Yet its dominance of the political stage has tended to reinforce these elements in our political culture and prevent the emergence of more ideological politics. Since Fianna Fáil basically set the ground rules since 1932, both Fine Gael and Labour have had to tailor themselves to be very odd partners in order to offer an alternative government. This has cloaked the fundamental differences in their political ideology.

The success of Fianna Fáil in setting the ground rules and in dominating the Irish political system demands closer analysis. Its success lies in its ability to maintain wide support from disadvantaged sectors of society, particularly small farmers and the working class, while serving the interests of both local and foreign business and large farmers. Through holding together these conflicting interests, its ability to win between 40% and 50% of the popular vote for over 50 years is a remarkable political achievement.

Rather than comparing it to any party in our neighbouring European countries, it is better understood by reference to parties such as Mexico's permanent ruling party, the PRI, Peru's APRA or Argentina's Peronists. As one Irishman living in Mexico once put it to me: 'Fianna Fáil and the PRI must be the capitalist world's two most successful political parties'.

Established around strong political leaders like Eamon de Valera, Haya de la Torre in Peru or Juan Domingo Perón in Argentina, these parties' rhetoric of radical change was quickly shown to cloak a fundamental conservatism. Instead of representing the interests of particular social classes, they claim to represent 'the nation' or 'the people'. They refuse to consider themselves political parties in the strict sense and emphasise their role as 'national movements' embracing the interests of all and alone offering the prospect of stability and national regeneration. Purporting to speak for all the people, they leave little room on the political stage for other parties to challenge them.

None of these parties allows wide-ranging debate on party policy which is made by the leadership for approval at closely controlled party conferences. But the leadership is also very responsive to grass-roots feeling within and outside the party and will seek to respond to it, though more often in form than in substance. When the party is in power the party faithful will always be amply rewarded for their loyalty.

This style of politics, usually known as populism, has the effect of preventing the emergence of strong movements of the oppressed, whether the working class or more marginalised sectors of the population. It is not surprising therefore that in the countries mentioned above, where strong populist parties have dominated the political stage in the twentieth century, the labour movement has been very effectively held in check by the dominant party.

It is only in the 1980s with the emergence of a strong people's movement that the dominance of these populist parties is being challenged in Latin America. The Peronists are already in decline while Mexico's PRI is having to resort to electoral fraud to remain in power.

But the Peruvian case is perhaps the most fascinating. There, because the military had always stepped in to prevent it taking power up to now, the populist APRA party got into government for the first time only in 1985, under the leadership of the charismatic Alan Garcia. Since then, however, its typically populist attempts to build a base of enduring support have failed because of the strength of the popular movement in the shanty towns. Instead, former supporters are deserting it for the left as they see it cannot deliver on its many promises. Of all these populist parties, Fianna Fáil seems the most enduring.

The Irish Left

In an article published in 1982, one of the country's leading political scientists, Tom Garvin of UCD, wrote that 'social and cultural change has outstripped the Irish political system's capacity to adapt, at least in the short run.'[2] The general election of 1987 which saw a fundamental re-alignment of Irish politics along class lines, indicates the beginnings of such adaptation. For the first time, the common interests of the conservative parties, 'now joined by the Progressive Democrats, was clearly seen. The emergence of the Workers Party and the steady growth of their parliamentary representation, on the other hand, has given a long-needed coherence to left-wing politics. Strengthened by the political quality of deputies such as Tony Gregory and Jim Kemmy, this new self-confident left is now challenging the Labour Party to opt for a real socialist alternative.

Such an alternative has a long way to go, however, before it can ever present a credible project for Irish society. Not the least of its problems is the continuing fragmentation of the Irish left, bitterly divided in particular by the ever-present 'national question'. Perhaps more disturbing is its failure to give coherence, leadership and direction to the marginalised at a time when they are being subjected to particularly harsh cutbacks in social services and in living standards. Instead of being able clearly to show up the way present government policies favour property owners, investors and large farmers while placing the burden of paying back our national debt on workers and the marginalised, the left have found themselves outflanked by the arch-politician Charles Haughey who has sold his policies as the only possible ones to stabilise the debt.

Lacking is any clear strategy on the part of the left or any process of developing detailed and credible policies embodying a real alternative for the future. It is particularly distressing, for example, that the left is showing no awareness of the debate raging in Latin America on alternative approaches towards debt repayment nor formulating credible alternatives for our situation. To some extent, this mirrors the left's relatively weak penetration of Irish society since it still has the allegiance of few academics and researchers, and therefore lacks the necessary ongoing groundwork on which to be able to develop policies. Secondly it mirrors the very inadequate attention given to creative and serious ideological debate aimed at interpreting our present impasse and offering new perspectives for future development.

In Latin America the growth of the people's movement has challenged the left to respond more creatively to the needs of the oppressed majority. Growing out of the widespread process of conscientisation and the creative new forms of organisation and mobilisation that resulted from it, the people's movement has given rise to new forms of social analysis rooted in the experience of the oppressed themselves. Strait-jacked in many countries by an over-rigid ideological reading of the political and economic situation, the left has been forced to come to terms with these more creative forms of social analysis.

In some countries this has led to the growth of new left-wing parties rooted firmly in the new mass movements. The best example of this is the Brazilian Workers' Party, founded in 1979 by left-wing militants many of whom had received their formation in the widespread network of Basic Christian Communities throughout Brazil. In others the traditional left has responded to the challenge of these new mass movements. In Peru, for example, the country's main left-wing parties formed the United Left coalition in 1980. Made up of eight parties as well as independent members, some of them prominent intellectuals and christians, this is now the country's main political opposition and has a good chance of winning the presidency in the 1990 elections.

The political importance of this cross-fertilisation between the new mass movements and the left, cannot be under-estimated. Since the 1970s, the left has appeared unable to offer a convincing alternative to the aggressive capitalist project of the new-right as symbolised by Reagan and Thatcher. The end of the post-war welfare state consensus in Western Europe has put the left on the defensive, unsure whether to accommodate itself to the more aggressive capitalism of the 1980s or to offer a more radical critique.

In Latin America, on the other hand, the left is articulating a far wider consensus, including the popular movement, sectors of the church, human rights groups, progressive intellectuals and artists. Unlike the Latin American left of the 1960s, based in many countries on small groups of middle class intellectuals, a new broad-based political movement is beginning to emerge in the late 1980s. Where the left has best responded to the challenge of the people's movement, it has been able to transcend the divisions inherited from imported versions of socialism, whether Communist, Trotskyist, Maoist or Social Democratic. What is emerging instead is a radical critique of the existing mechanisms of exploitation and domination to which the masses of the oppressed can relate. It is not too much to call this the seeds of an alternative socialist culture.

While Mikhail Gorbachev in the Soviet Union and Deng Xiaoping in China are engaged in one attempt to re-define socialism within the socialist camp, the new mass movements in Latin America are also giving birth to a new socialist project. But, unlike the Soviet Union or China, this has not emerged from the centres of power but rather from the new phenomenon of the masses becoming aware and mobilising. It thus promises to be more deeply-rooted and enduring and is full of hopeful possibilities for radical political, economic and social transformation.

While we use democracy to refer to a particular political system, it can also refer to the values and outlook of a culture. In this sense Latin America, despite its many military dictatorships and authoritarian regimes, is a far more democratic place than is Ireland. What the last twenty years have seen happen throughout the sub-continent is that poor and oppressed people have begun to take power into their own hands and fashion their own democratic structures at grass-roots level. Breaking out of their traditional marginalisation, therefore, they have become a force to be reckoned with in society.

Irish society urgently needs a similar process of solidarity strong enough to withstand the pressures of a highly individualistic society. The poor need to be helped mobilise together around issues that really matter to them, to make their voices heard and to become actors on the stage of Irish society from which they have for far too long been excluded.

CHAPTER 7

Resources for Change: Culture

For anyone who has lived in Latin America, returning to Ireland involves a major culture shock. While you do not immediately encounter the same extremes of flaunted wealth and grinding poverty, neither do you come across the same sense of struggle and hope that so characterises Latin America today. It is these qualities that make even a short stay in Latin America such an invigorating experience for Irish people. Based upon the poor taking power into their own hands and confronting their problems with creativity and resourcefulness, this sense of struggle and hope is infectious.

Behind it lies a fundamental shift of consciousness, the move from inferiority to equality, from imitation to creativity, from submissiveness to dignity. Ever since the beginning of colonialism with the arrival of Spanish and Portuguese conquerers in the sixteenth century, Latin American societies had been relegated to a position of inferiority, forced to imitate the mores and culture of the 'mother country' and drained of any last spark of dignity and self-worth.

A very similar process happened to us Irish – it may have taken longer to achieve our submission but the end result was very similar. Political independence in Latin America (as in Ireland) did very little to change that situation. The overt political structures of colonialism may have come to an end but the reality remained with the United States overtaking even Britain as the world's major colonial power.

Cultural colonialism
One of the traits that appear to be common to peoples who were colonised is an inferiority complex, a lack of pride in themselves, an inability to affirm their own distinctiveness.

Some countries, like India, experienced colonialism for only a relatively short historical period and in a way that did not destroy the native civilisation or cultural institutions. For others it was a far more brutal and destructive experience, obliterating whole civilisations and reducing races to subjugation. In this regard both Ireland and the countries of Latin America have had a similar historical experience. Both today bear similar psychological and cultural traits, the legacy of cultural colonialism.

In an interview he gave to the Lima-based *Noticias Aliadas,* the well-known Uruguayan journalist and writer, Eduardo Galeano, summed up this legacy as it is experienced in Latin America:

> I think Latin America is gravely ill with alienation; it sees itself through the eyes of those who exploit and oppress it. Latin America has been trained in resignation and fear; it has been taught to betray itself.
>
> Under-development is a structure of powerlessness; it is much more than what the figures say it is; it is a sinister, dark and highly complicated mechanism that leads certain countries, poorly named the 'Third World,' to deny their very identity. These countries are caged in so they can't think with their own heads, feel with their own hearts or walk with their own legs. As a result they are in danger of aping others, of automatically importing foreign ways of thinking.[1]

Though we Irish may be little aware of it, there is much in our culture that could be similarly described. The most revealing symptom is the degree to which we copy from abroad, a process completely different to allowing trends and ideas from abroad to interact with our own approaches, thus broadening and enriching them. Instead, in everything from town planning to economic policies, from media to religion, we simply import for the most part what is done elsewhere and copy it here. In the process we pay little attention to the fact that the countries from which we import – Britain, the United States, West Germany and other EEC countries – are the countries of the world perhaps most dissimilar to us, our history and our present-day problems. If we have to copy, it would at least make sense to copy from those exploited, post-colonial countries most like ourselves, situated in the so-called Third World.

We copy others because we cannot, in Galeano's words, think with our own heads, feel with our own hearts or walk with our own legs. Striking indeed in Ireland is the degree to which we fail to reflect on our own reality, to acknowledge our distinctive historical experience and to bring any sophistication to bear on the task of evolving strategies for change. Ireland today often strikes the observer like a person who has lost touch with their own background, who has no direction in life and therefore who wanders aimlessly, prey to easy manipulation and to passing fads.

The legacy of cultural colonialism is an aspect of our national life that is largely overlooked or even denied. For those whose primary concern is to provide jobs or to combat the growing poverty in our society, such concerns appear esoteric and irrelevant. The lessons of Nicaragua are instructive in this regard.

Nicaragua: Discovering Dignity

In July 1986, Eduardo Galeano paid a visit to Nicaragua. In a long article written afterwards, he identified the re-discovery of dignity as the most important characteristic of the Nicaraguan revolution. It is a point we in the West, obsessed as we are with material progress, can easily miss.

Galeano writes:

> One Contra chief defined Nicaragua as the country where 'there isn't any'; and he is right. The Revolution has an abundance of moral authority, dignity, creative enthusiasm – everything that the Contras' millions cannot buy. But it lacks parts, medicines, clothing and the basic ingredients for the basic meal: oil, rice, beans and corn. Everyone complains, and they do it loudly. The economic hardships are discouring and wear down energies. The war has reached the kitchen table and seeped into the last corner of every house.[2]

Having identified dignity and creative enthusiasm as the

heart of what the revolution has given the Nicaraguan people, Galeano goes on to point out how these are precisely what the powerful of the world want to stifle. 'Third World people are condemned to copy; they have the right to be an echo but not a voice,' he writes.[3] As long as Nicaragua copied the United States and obediently submitted to its view of the world, it was favoured. When it dared to break free of that, to try to fashion something entirely new in order to provide a decent livelihood for all its people, it found its right to exist was taken from it by the most powerful nation on earth. It is vilified as a Soviet and Cuban pawn; its leaders are accused of being totalitarian.

Galeano admits the Sandinistas have made mistakes. 'Inevitably, numerous mistakes are committed by a colonised country when it decides to become a real nation, stands up on its own two feet, and begins to walk, stumbling, without the crutch of imperialism. It is well known that under-development implies a tradition of inefficiency and ignorance, a fatalistic acceptance of powerlessness as one's natural destiny. It is very difficult to escape from this trap, but it is not impossible,' he writes.[4]

It is Nicaragua's determination to escape from this trap that excites and encourages so many oppressed peoples throughout the world. Even more than the revolution's successes in re-distributing wealth, in providing health care and education for all the people and in fashioning new structures of political participation, what impresses the observer is the new sense of pride that the people have, particularly the poor and marginalised people, in themselves and their country.

This pride was very evident during the 1980 literacy campaign when old and poor people, who could never have dared dream that one day they could read and write, succeeded in doing that in just five months. Similarly, in the many assemblies around the country where ordinary people get the opportunity to discuss openly and air their criticisms freely with senior government ministers, including the president himself, the sense of new-found dignity is unmistakable. For the first time, not only in their lives but in the history of their country, ordinary people, the poor and deprived masses, are being shown that they are important, that their contribution to the life of the country is being valued.

The best efforts of the Sandinista government to implement revolutionary programmes among the Indian peoples of the country's Atlantic Coast proved ineffective until their cultural rights were guaranteed to them. Ray Hooker, a senior member of the Nicaraguan parliament from the Atlantic Coast and also national co-ordinator of the commission that drew up the law granting semi-autonomy to the region, explained to me the importance of such rights:

> By cultural rights we are talking about establishing an environment in which our different Indian peoples can be proud of their own identity instead of being ashamed as they used to be before. This is absolutely essential because in meaningful social transformation self-pride plays a very important role. Without it no such transformation can take place in people who have been historically oppressed, who have been second-class citizens.
>
> Each human being has access to the pool of creativity that is naturally within them to the degree that self-pride is part of their make-up. If each human being, or if a whole people, are afflicted by a massive inferiority complex (which is what happens to people who have been historically oppressed), then they have no access to the pools of creativity present within them. Self-pride is like the key that opens the door to creativity and it is creativity which we must use to go about really building a new society. This is where the exercise of cultural rights is so important.[5]

The rights to which Hooker is referring include the education of children through their first language and the learning of the national language, Spanish, only as a single subject on the curriculum instead of learning everything through Spanish as before. Referring to the Miskito peoples, the largest cultural minority in Nicaragua, Hooker says that 'for the first time in history, the Miskito child is learning that to be Miskito is as important as to be Spanish-speaking and to be Spanish-speaking is not more important than to be Miskito.'

It remains to be seen how effective will such measures be in instilling self-pride into a particularly marginalised minority. What is important, however, is the recognition by a revolutionary government that political participation or economic restructuring is not enough.

It is in Nicaragua and Cuba that I have experienced this sense of dignity in an almost palpable way. Visiting Havana, for example, one has the regular experience of local people coming up to you on the buses, in restaurants, on the street in order proudly to tell you what the revolution and Fidel have done for them. While a similar sense of dignity can be found among those actively involved in action for change in other Latin American countries, it is not at all as widespread among the general population. Very evident still is that inefficiency and ignorance, that acceptance of powerlessness that Galeano identifies as some of the traits of under-development.

Repossessing Ireland

A movement with the potential to challenge the roots of our national malaise and offer an essential element for the creation of a sense of pride in ourselves and a new vision for the future, is the Irish language movement. This is not a recent arrival on the Irish stage. In the eyes of some it would be identified as part of the sterile status quo but that is to misunderstand its more dynamic elements. Its potential as a cultural movement out of which grew a new political consciousness was seen at the turn of the century but that new consciousness was quickly crushed within the constraints of the twenty-six county state.

Máirtín Ó Cadhain is the movement's towering figure this century as well as one of Ireland's greatest creative writers. He brought a sense of energy, penetrating analysis and radical vision to a movement that had been domesticated by the debilitating embrace of the twenty-six county establishment. For Ó Cadhain, the attempt to save the national language from extinction embodied and expressed nothing less than the attempt to take control again of our country, to repossess it. As he put it in his much quoted phrase: *Sí an Ghaeilge athghabháil na hÉireann agus is í athghabháil na hÉireann slanú na Gaeilge.*[6]

In August 1969, just over a year before his death, Ó Cadhain gave a lecture in which he expressed his vision for the language movement. In this lecture, published afterwards under the title 'Gluaiseacht na Gaeilge, Gluaiseacht ar Strae', Ó Cadhain situates the language at the heart of the movement for radical social, economic, political and cultural change in Ireland. *Ní hé amháin gur cóir do lucht na Gaeilge a bheith páirteach i gcoga seo Athghabhála na hÉireann – is é an t-aon rud é ar fiú a bheith páirteach ann in Éirinn – ach is é ár ndualgas a bheith dhá chinnireacht agus dhá threorú. Bíodh an Ghaeilge ag stiúra na réabhlóide, ar an gcaoi seo bíodh an Ghaeilge ar na smaointí is forásaí in Éirinn.*[7] Where the challenge of the poor and the weak against wealth and injustice is strongest, he writes, there is the natural place for Irish to be spoken, for the language to come into its own.

Ó Cadhain turned his searing criticism against Fianna Fáil *agus dá leithéidí eile.* The only thing Irish can expect under Fianna Fáil is death, he declared. For him the aim is nothing less than to take Ireland from the hands of Fianna Fáil and their likes and give it back to the people – *seilbh na hÉireann agus a cuid maoine uilig a thabhairt ar ais do mhuintir na hÉireann.*[8] For this reason, he says: *Sé dualgas lucht na Gaeilge a bheith ina sóisialaigh.*[9] He goes on to say that he saw class distinction and class warfare at work in the Conamara Gaeltacht were he grew up long before he read James Connolly and Karl Marx's *Das Kapital.* From his own Gaeltacht experience, he says, *gheobhadh Marx, Engels agus Lenin cruthú breá ann ar a ndeimhne gurb iad an ardaicme agus lucht an rachmais, na* capitalists, *is túisce a thréigeas saíúlacht nó cultúr na muintire.*[10]

In this lecture, Ó Cadhain urges new forms of creative protest, from sit-ins to pickets, active resistance to passive resistance. Some of the ways he outlines have been used to great effect by other groups, for example by the peace women at the time of the Reagan visit in 1984. He urges publishing scandals involving government ministers, setting up an underground radio, taking part in elections, establishing an Irish-speaking dormitory town close to Dublin, a town that would train young Irish-speaking cadres for the revolution, as he puts it idealistically.

Ó Cadhain was no simple theorist. Though he ended his days as professor of Irish in Trinity College, he never lost his radical activism. Through the movement 'Misneach' in the mid 1960s, he helped to put into practice some of his ideas about more militant protest actions. But, more importantly, he inspired younger members of the language movement and under his influence grew a Gaeltacht civil rights movement. One of the movement's major victories was the establishment of Raidió na Gaeltachta in 1972 following the success of the illegal Saor-Raidió Chonamara. The coming on the air in late 1987 of a pirate Gaeltacht television service and the government's subsequent allocation of money from the National Lottery to fund a pilot service, looks set to repeat the earlier success.

Far more important for the future of the language and its function as a crucial element in the national psyche is the growth of an Irish-speaking population particularly in the Dublin area. While most of the Gaeltachtaí continue to decline, there has been a steady increase in the number of Irish-speaking kindergarten and primary schools being set up with the support of parents. More young parents are now raising their children bilingually or in Irish than before. The number of books being published in Irish has increased from around 40 a year 10 years ago to around 150 every year now. New pubs and clubs in Irish witness to the vigour of the language. Alongside this must also be added the new sense of pride in their identity as a cultural minority evident in some

Gaeltacht areas.

Such hopeful developments are all the result of grass-roots initiatives, often in the face of active state opposition. It is the umbilical cord linking the language movement to state support which continues to kill it. For, while activists lament the growing marginalisation of Irish in the educational system and the lack of any evident government commitment to it, they still depend on the government for grants and hand-outs. Indeed Roinn na Gaeltachta does little else but administer such grants.

It must be plainly evident after 65 years of state financial support that money will not save the Irish language. The key step urgently needed if Irish is not to die out as the vernacular language of some living community somewhere in the country is the establishment of an Irish-speaking town or suburb. This aim has been formulated in various ways by such people as Máirtín Ó Cadhain, Deasún Fennell and Liam Mac Mathúna in his collection of essays *Pobal na Gaeilge.*[11] It has been shown to be feasible. Yet, for all their stated love of the language, activists have been as yet unable to take even the first steps towards its implementation.

Ireland today is a bilingual country but, as with so much else about ourselves, we fail to acknowledge this in our national life. Even cursory listening to Raidió na Gaeltachta quickly indicates just how widespread is the ability to use Irish and to deal with contemporary experience and events through Irish. The success of Lá na Gaeilge and the widespread attempts made by people to use even the little Irish they have indicate the extent of goodwill that can be built upon. Yet, this ability remains passive in our national life reflecting again our inability to relate to the potential among ourselves.

If Ireland is to build any future for itself, the language will be an essential element in fashioning a new and dignified image of ourselves. Any fundamental breakthrough to real self-awareness and creativity cannot take place without it. The remarkable growth and creativity in Irish music over the past two decades indicates the potential for such a breakthrough.

As Diarmuid Ó Donnchadha of Gael Linn put it to me, as long as we are speaking English we see ourselves as being on the edge of the English-speaking world, dependent on others for our future. Those of us who speak Irish see ourselves as being at the heart of our world and it is up to us to build a better world out of our own resources and abilities.

As long as the language is viewed as something apart, almost like an ancient manuscript that must be preserved, then it is bound to die. Irish can only find itself again as part of a broader counter-culture, concerned not about its own survival but about our common survival as a vital human community. We are fast becoming a dormitory country for the central economies of the EEC and North America, raising our children and caring for our old but seeing our best educated young going abroad to work. At home, the same trends are marginalising more and more of our people, relegating them to depend on meagre social welfare while a small elite grows rich as part of an international 'jet-set'. Concern for our survival as a people is just as urgent as concern for the survival of our language.

'Hidden Energies'

The basis of all social transformation lies in the ability of an oppressed people to affirm their own identity and their own history, to discover a pride and a dignity in themselves. This alone can unlock the pools of creativity in each of us. While there may be many differences between us Irish and Latin Americans, the fundamental task of self-affirmation is one still awaiting us.

Galeano, in the interview already quoted, agrees with this need to help the peoples of Latin America discover themselves, their own hidden identity. Indeed his work as a writer and journalist is largely devoted to trying to discover what he calls 'the secret energies that urge us to create'.[12] The process of political decolonisation, begun when the countries of Latin America gained independence at the beginning of the nineteenth century, was taken over by 'merchants, shysters, generals and landowners, says Galeano. 'Their appropriation of the continent's independence drove us toward forms of alienation and colonialism I believe are worse than the ones Latin America endured before its independence. There is a long history of racism and elitism that negates the wellsprings of awareness that are indispensable for all of us born on this soil.'

In Ireland, too, much of the potential of the process of decolonisation begun at the end of the last century in the cultural revolution expressed in such organisations as the GAA, Conradh na Gaeilge and the Abbey Theatre, was quickly dissipated by the infighting of different groups of the middle classes. Ireland, too, has suffered profoundly from a history of elitism and sectarianism that has negated our wellsprings of awareness.

Galeano, in his work, seeks to discover those muffled voices that have never been allowed to shout at the top of their lungs. . . those voices which have for so long been strangled, negated and manipulated. These are the voices of 'the outcast, the despised, the ignorant,' he says, and he outlines the message we get from these ancient and despised voices. 'It is not one of greed or of private property, Rather, it's a message of solidarity, of collective ownership, of life in community.'

Galeano is not trying to re-create some idyllic past to which he is urging a return. Rather, he is urgently trying to recover a tradition, to discover that tradition's energies and to release these for the tasks of cultural affirmation, of social transformation. As he says at the end of his *Noticias Aliadas* interview: 'Latin America is a region in search of itself: it will discover itself only very slowly, and make many errors along the way. But isn't it better to make mistakes on the road than not to travel at all?'

While the struggles against political colonialism are largely finished throughout the world, peoples are only painfully becoming aware of the continuing hold of colonialism on their culture and their very minds. This hold, which grows ever more sophisticated with the advent of instant satellite communications, has to be challenged before there is any hope of a more peaceful and just world. Many Third World peoples are beginning to challenge it in different ways. We in Ireland urgently need to discover our ways of challenging it and of fashioning our own future for ourselves.

CHAPTER 8

Has Ireland a Future?
Jobs and Growth

Even before independence in 1921, Irish people had come to accept our economic backwardness as normal. With few exceptions, therefore, the movement for independence was not characterised by any radical economic vision and the economic policies of the Cumann na nGaedheal government during the first decade of the Free State were conservative in the extreme. Though De Valera's economic approach when he took office in 1932 was based on a coherent vision of a self-sufficient island, his innate conservatism and caution in economic affairs meant that his efforts were doomed to failure.

He made no attempt to control the outflow of Irish capital which preferred the more secure return offered by investment in Britain and elsewhere. Neither did he seek to encourage the development of a strong exporting sector by the new native industries established as a result of his protectionist policies. The legacy of these two failures is still very much with us in the 1980s as large outflows of capital continue and we have yet to build up strong Irish manufacturing industries capable of securing export markets.

Poor economic growth resulting in low living standards and high emigration came to seem the norm for many Irish people. The sudden surge of prosperity associated with the new reliance on foreign capital in the 1960s challenged, therefore, long-established expectations. But as we look back now, we can see that while those deeply rooted traditional expectations may have changed somewhat in the 1960s and 1970s, they quickly re-asserted themselves when economic decline set in in the early 1980s. Instead of leading to widespread political demands for a change in economic policy, Irish people returned to the practice of voting with their feet and looking for work elsewhere. Between 1981 and 1987, it is estimated that as many as a quarter of a million may have left the country in search of work.

Underlying these traditional expectations is the sense that sustained economic growth is not possible in Ireland. Such a sense is not surprising given the cautious and unimaginative economic strategies of successive governments. With a few exceptions, Irish economists have also failed to explore alternatives and stimulate public debate on them. Neither has the general public ever shown itself interested in such debate. The result, both at the level of theory and policy, has been the dominance of a narrow economic orthodoxy remarkably resistant to public challenge or accountability. It is little wonder that we have come to accept economic stagnation as somehow our divinely-ordained lot.

A New Economic Model

Surprising as it may seem to the general public who hear little about it through our media, a consensus has been growing over recent years around an alternative economic strategy for a post-colonial, under-developed economy like ours. This new approach is often linked to the study of the Irish economy done by the Telesis Consultancy Group for the National Economic and Social Council (NESC) which was released in February 1982. Its main recommendations were endorsed by the NESC, an advisory council made up of government, trade union, farming and employers representatives. The strategy recommended by Telesis was also subsequently supported by the Irish Congress of Trade Unions in its Framework for a National Plan, entitled 'Confronting the Jobs Crisis'.

Underlying this new consensus is a growing awareness of the failure of multinational companies to fuel growth throughout the economy. While the multinationals here are achieving high growth rates for themselves, they are providing relatively few jobs, are largely divorced from the rest of the economy and are proving very expensive for the state. In the light of this failure, a new strategy is needed which could give better value for money and offer the prospect of creating large numbers of sustainable jobs over the longer term.

As important as value for money, however, the aim would be to build up strong industries under Irish control which would stimulate other sectors of the economy through using a high level of Irish-made inputs. The key to the success of this strategy would be the ability to capture and maintain markets overseas. This, therefore, would require careful selection of types of industry for which there would be demand abroad and which could be developed in Ireland.

Such a strategy would demand a collaborative effort between the state and private enterprise to concentrate on building up such large-scale Irish industries. These could be consortia of private and state firms or could be a large private or state enterprise. They would need not just generous grants to support them in the initial phase but also assistance in marketing, in product research, in managerial and labour skills. All of this capability already exists in the Irish economy; what would be needed would be clearer planning and the identification of key industries with export potential.

Dr Eoin O'Malley of the ESRI has identified different sectors of the engineering industry as being most suitable for this sort of development, including agricultural machinery, process plants for the food industry, precision tool-making, medical instruments and the like. Taking the example of bicycles, he says that such an industry could be developed in different phases with the eventual aim of creating a large company producing different types of bicycle for which all the parts would also be made in Ireland.[1]

To back up his contention that there is room for developing such large companies, he points to the fact that Ireland already has a robust engineering industry, in which the number of firms doubled from 800 to 1,600 between 1973 and 1983. However, most of these are very small and unable to spend much on the necessary research and development if they are to develop further. The skills and entrepreneurship are there, says O'Malley, but they need to be developed in a planned way as large companies or consortia so that they can capture export markets and lead to knock-on effects in other sectors of the economy.

Paradoxically, this strategy is based, not on the example of any socialist country, but of Japan. An under-developed Third World country thirty years ago, Japan has become one of the world's industrial giants through just such a process of careful planning and judicious protection of weak industries until such a time as they could compete successfully with the products of the United States and Western Europe. One of the world's great capitalist show-cases, Japan did this through active state involvement in the economy channelling resources in a planned and efficient way. More recently, this approach has seen South Korea, Taiwan and Singapore make similar strides forward. Just as the 1964 Olympic Games in Tokyo signified Japan's new self-confidence on the world stage, so too the 1988 Olympics are signifying South Korea's new world stature.

Instead of following such a strategy, successive Irish governments have failed to face the underlying challenge posed by our economic under-development. They prefer to follow the example of our nearest neighbours, diagnosing our failure to create more jobs as deriving from the lack of sufficient incentives for the private sector or from too much state interference in the economy. Withdraw the state from the market place, reduce taxes on industry and keep labour costs down, they argue, and the private sector will begin to invest and create more jobs.

Budgetary strategy has consistently expressed this faith in the capacity of private enterprise. The 1988 budget, for example, saw those companies earning high profits, such as the banks, gain further tax relief through changes in corporation tax while no attempt was made to raise further revenue through increasing Ireland's very low taxes on wealth and property. Central to that budget's strategy was the lowering of interest rates, making it easier for companies to borrow. Yet, as the Jesuit Centre for Faith and Justice pointed out in its reaction to the budget 'cheaper capital can lead to labour-substituting investment as much as to labour-needing investment.'[2] The lesson of some Irish entrepreneurs shows also that cheaper capital here simply leads them to invest abroad, so that the jobs are created elsewhere.

While factors such as interest rates and levels of taxation undoubtedly play some role, exclusive concentration on them overlooks the fact that Ireland is not a developed industrial economy like Britain, the United States or West Germany. These countries have a robust private industrial sector which has the capacity to avail of free-market conditions to expand and create more jobs. In Ireland, private industry has for the most part proved too weak to avail of the challenges of open competition. Even at the height of our recent industrial growth, between 1973 and 1980, more jobs were lost in Irish manufacturing companies than were created, with a net loss for those years of 2,258 jobs. With the economic decline since 1980 and growing unemployment, this figure has increased dramatically. As the Jesuit Centre added in the statement already quoted above: 'Nothing in our recent history should lead us to expect the Irish private sector on its own to create jobs on the scale required.'[3]

Meanwhile Fianna Fáil promises to develop our natural resources of land, sea and forestry to provide more jobs. These are certainly important resources with the potential to create a lot of wealth and jobs in Ireland. Yet, even the government's own targets for job creation in this area are relatively modest. Mr Haughey has admitted, for example, that in food-processing, the area with most potential for job creation, he hopes for 5,000 new jobs to be created by 1992. Another change in government strategy over recent years which is to be welcomed is the greater concentration of the IDA's resources in supporting small Irish industries. Here also, however, the potential for job creation is extremely small compared to the scale of the problem.

It is clear, therefore, that a new strategy is urgently needed. The various political parties of the left, the Labour Party, the Workers Party and the Democratic Socialist Party all espouse a strategy broadly similar to that outlined above. The setting up of the National Development Corporation by the 1982-87 coalition government, on the insistence on the Labour Party, created one of the necessary instruments for implementing this alternative strategy. Yet, in the 1988 budget, the NDC received a paltry £700,000.

Inevitably, there are risks associated with a major change in government strategy. But, comparing the huge resources devoted to the present strategy with the meagre and insecure results, it must be obvious that such risks are worth taking. As Dr O'Malley has written: 'While there will inevitably be caution about any major new policy departure, it is also inevitable that major new departures have to be contemplated if we want results which differ quite radically from past experience.'[4]

Developing Agriculture

No matter how successful any new strategy for industrial development in Ireland, its impact will be limited unless present trends in agriculture are radically reversed. Both in terms of numbers employed and its contribution to Gross National Product, agriculture occupies a much larger place in the Irish economy than it does in almost any other EEC country. This aspect too, makes us similar to a Third World country.

If the struggles of the nineteenth century were concentrated on gaining possession of the land, the trends of the late twentieth century are steadily depopulating the countryside and concentrating land ownership yet again. In 1960 there were 250,000 farmers in Ireland, but by the late 1980s this had fallen to 170,000. Under current EEC plans, this number is due to halve over the next decade. This rural depopulation puts further pressure on urban jobs and services and swells the tide of emigration.

These trends characterise the Third World as a whole as agriculture is transformed into big business benefiting the larger farmers or, in many cases, foreign multinationals. Paradoxically, in this situation, more intensive exploitation of the land results not in more jobs for rural families but in their expulsion from the land to make way for mechanised, high-capital agri-business. Throughout the Third World, this has led to mass migration to the cities and increased malnutrition as food grown for export replaces the subsistence crops grown to feed the local people.

This transformation of agriculture into big business lies behind the current crisis in Irish agriculture. As small farmers are being forced to leave the land, large farmers are paid generous grants and subsidies to exploit their land intensively. Added to these direct subsidies and grants is the indirect subsidy paid to farmers by consumers who have to pay over twice the world price for their food products.

This policy results in ever declining numbers of farmers growing so much unwanted food that increasing amounts of it have to be stored every year. The costs of storing this food surplus alone eat up half the total agricultural budget of the EEC. Meanwhile 55% of Irish farmers are classified as marginal and receive little support under this policy. All it offers them is encouragement to leave the land altogether. As the architect of this policy, Dr Sicco Mansholt, said of the present situation: 'My fear is that my dream of 30 years ago will be ruined if we go on as we are.'[5]

As the first EEC Agriculture Commissioner, Mansholt's dream was an EEC of productive and prosperous farmers, guaranteed a reasonable income as a protection against the vagaries of the weather. By now, however, the dream has turned into a nightmare. In Ireland it has led to a prosperous livelihood for about 30% of farmers while 70% have not only to live on incomes well below the averages for urban workers but face pressures to leave the land altogether.

To return to Mansholt's dream will mean a drastic revision

of current policies, directing credit and support not just to the larger farmers from whom an economic return can be expected, but also to the smaller farmers. Better planning in this sector should be able to develop a robust small farming industry, supplying the Irish market with fresh and quality horticultural products, much of which are currently imported. Furthermore, with increasing evidence of the damage being done to our soil, our wildlife and our food chain by the over-intensive use of fertilisers and growth hormones in cattle, the state should channel more resources towards natural forms of growing food. With good marketing techniques, such food could capture a stable export market.

Paying Back our Debt

The burden of Ireland's huge national debt hangs over all attempts at forging a new strategy to develop our economic potential. Paradoxically, it is the very party which landed us in the mess in the first place which is now taking decisive measures to get us out of it. The measures chosen by the Haughey administration in 1987, including major cutbacks in government social spending, reductions in the numbers of public officials and strict adherence to free-market policies, follow closely those austerity packages forced on Latin American debtor countries by the International Monetary Fund (IMF).

Like the Irish Taoiseach, Latin American presidents sold these policies to their electorates as being the only possible remedy. The alternative, they said, was economic catastrophe. Within a few short years, however, by the mid-1980s they were having to face the fact that these policies were themselves causing an economic and social catastrophe so severe as to plunge Latin America into its worst economic crisis ever.

In Peru, for example, manufacturing industry, which accounts for over 20% of GDP, saw its output fall by more than a fifth between 1981 and 1983; by 1984 it was operating at only 40% of capacity. Despite generous tax incentives, multinational investment increased only briefly and by 1984 more dollars were being repatriated from Peru than were entering in new investment. State enterprises were run down through lack of investment, adding further to the economic decline.

The social effects were grim. The impact of austerity measures in 1983 alone led to a 20% fall in real wages that year. A World Bank report in 1985 concluded that 'the overwhelming majority of Peruvians are markedly worse off than in 1970'. In the ten years from 1973 to 1983, the average employed worker lost close to 60% of buying power while the number of fully employed workers dropped from 50% to 37% of the workforce. Yet this strategy did nothing to help the government pay back its US$14bn debt. So severely had these policies hit the economy that when Alan Garcia became president in 1985, it was estimated that debt repayments for the year totalled 160% of the total value of Peru's exports!

Peru is no exception in Latin America. These austerity policies have had a disastrous effect on economic performance as well as on social services and living standards in every country of the region. This has forced many governments to the conclusion expressed by the conservative President José Sarney of Brazil in his 1985 address to the UN General Assembly, that the debt cannot be paid back at the expense of the misery and hunger of the poor.

Or, as Cardinal Paulo Evaristo Arns of São Paulo, Brazil, put it in a much-quoted letter to an international conference on the debt problem held in Havana, Cuba, in August 1985: 'What is at risk here is not the accounts of international creditors, but rather the lives of millions of people who cannot suffer the permanent threat of regressive measures and unemployment which bring misery and death.'

A new consensus now exists among Latin American leaders that the only way to repay their debts is through economic growth. Some have unilaterally decided to limit their debt repayments in the hope of using the money they save this way to stimulate economic growth. Peru has limited its repayments to 10% of its export earnings, thus directly linking its repayments to its economic growth rate; the more it grows, the more it will pay back. Other countries, including Brazil, Argentina and Mexico, the three largest debtors, have held out for far more advantageous terms in re-negotiations of their debts. Underlying all these different means is the common end of economic growth.

Though the structure of the Irish debt is very different to that of Latin America, the basic principle of economic growth should also apply here. The current austerity policies of the Fianna Fáil government may boost profits for certain enterprises, particularly the multinationals, but even the government admits that the economy will remain stagnant for some years to come. The act of faith they make that reducing the debt burden now will somehow lead to economic growth in the future was found by all Latin American governments to be a disastrous illusion, setting back their economies a decade or more and leading to great hardship for most of their people. We in Ireland should learn from their mistakes.

What is particularly disturbing here is the lack of research into alternative strategies for limiting debt repayment. Raymond Crotty is one of the few economists to have faced the seriousness of the problem and to have clearly stated that, in the long run, the debt is simply unpayable. His recommendation to repudiate the debt altogether, however, under-estimates the possibility of retaliatory action by the international community and also neglects the fact that over 60% of our debt is domestic and not foreign. Repudiation of our domestic debt would, therefore, wipe out the savings of many ordinary Irish people. While his attention to the problem is salutary, his recommendations need more debate and refinement by economists, to say the least.

There is, however, much to be learned from the various efforts being made by many debtor countries to limit their repayments. One of the basic lessons learned by Third World debtors is that if they stand united they pose a threat to the international financial system and are in a stronger bargaining position, whereas divided they are extremely dependent on their creditors. Ireland should also take this lesson to heart and take an active part in international discussions by debtor countries.

Ireland would even be well-placed to take the initiative of creating some global network of the debtor countries to co-ordinate common positions in negotiations with creditors. While this country would have little to benefit from certain of the ideas being discussed among debtor countries, such as an outright moratorium as declared for three years by African countries or limiting repayment to a percentage of export earnings, we would greatly benefit from others, such as fixing low interest rates for debt repayments. Another idea currently in favour among some debtor countries is swopping portions of the foreign debt for equity shares in local industry; such an arrangement might be of benefit to the IDA in dealings with certain multinationals. More important, such an approach might be applicable in the case of our domestic debt.

Apart from mechanisms to facilitate less onerous repayment of the debt, international discussions among debtors have focused on issues such as fairer trading relationships between the Northern 'developed' countries and the Southern 'under-developed' ones. Since Ireland in many ways belongs to the latter grouping, such discussions are ones in which we should take an active interest. Our membership of the EEC may limit our freedom of action in this regard, as the EEC is itself responsible for undermining the exports of Third World countries particularly through its extensive subsidies of farm produce.

In the long run, however, Ireland should take a larger view of such issues not motivated by immediate self-interest. There would be much to be gained both politically and economically if Ireland were to become a voice within the EEC for the radical reform of its policies to ensure greater equity to the Third World. Ireland could seek to develop a block of the smaller EEC countries with progressive Third World policies, such as Greece and Denmark, to support such a stand. Some argue that Ireland should withdraw from the EEC altogether but that might be a recipe for isolationism more than for development.

Department of Finance officials baulk at any moves that might damage Ireland's high credit rating internationally. Since we are able to repay our debt, they argue, then we should do so faithfully. The point comes, however, when the question has to be asked whether continuing repayment is worth the economic decline and social hardship caused as a result. Far more beneficial in the long run would be to throw our lot in with other debtor countries in the demand for some reduction of the overall debt burden.

As US economist Susan George pointed out at a major international debt conference in Lima, Peru, in January 1988, the Third World's total global indebtedness is around $1 trillion, equal to the amount lost by the US Stock Exchange on Black Monday, 19 October 1987. If such a loss could be borne by the international financial system, so too could much of the international debt be written off, argued George. Ireland will look foolish indeed if it continues faithfully re-paying its debt at great cost to the poor at home, only to find other large debtors having their debts reduced or written off due to international pressure.

Protecting the Weak

Apart from the particular problems faced by the Irish economy – its failure to develop its full potential and its heavy indebtedness – Ireland also faces the contemporary problems associated with the fast pace at which technology is replacing human labour. This has severely affected employment in many economies with economists and sociologists arguing that it is no longer possible to imagine an era of full employment again. Even in the socialist countries where full employment has been guaranteed, measures being taken to modernise the economy seem inevitably to lead to the emergence of unemployment. While the debate on these issues is far from concluded, what it does appear to underline are the limits of industrial development today. If the era of full employment is gone for ever, society must find more adequate ways of supporting those to whom it cannot offer a job in the traditional sense.

In this regard, our social welfare system is far from adequate. It has grown up piecemeal with new benefits being added on as new needs arose. The end result is a cumbersome and complicated system with payments in most cases too low to cover basic needs. But, more importantly, the system is not designed for a situation in which many people are permanently unemployed. Even if employees have paid their social insurance, they are still only entitled to receive for a limited period the unemployment benefit to which they have contributed. Furthermore, such regulations as signing on in person every week and being unable to study while receiving unemployment assistance since one would not be available for work, are designed for a situation in which unemployment is temporary. If society cannot guarantee work to its citizens, then it should guarantee everyone a minimum income adequate to cover their basic needs. Such a demand is now the stated policy of groups as diverse as the Workers Party and the Catholic church's Conference of Major Religious Superiors (CMRS) which represents all religious orders in Ireland. People should receive this income as a right and not be made to feel that there is a stigma attached to receiving it. Equally importantly, the receipt of such a minimum income should in no way prevent people from advancing themselves through education, or from taking part-time work when it becomes available. Rather, such initiative should be encouraged by the system.

Again, such a possibility is by no means utopian. The Commission on Social Welfare which published its comprehensive examination of the social welfare system in July 1986 made similar recommendations, though it stopped short of recommending a minimum income for all. What it did recommend, however, is that the system be greatly simplified and that payment levels be related to 'a level of income which would be sufficient to maintain a single adult in independent circumstances where there is no additional source of income, at a standard which is linked to living standards in society generally'. This, it calculated, would mean substantial increases in present levels of social welfare benefits. While welcoming these proposals, the government's response was to plead inability to pay. The commission's report calculated that it would cost £560 million to implement, but showed how £226 million could be raised by expanding the system of Pay-Related Social Insurance (PRSI).

What this response showed, however, was just how low the poor come on the government's order of priorities. There are alternative sources of taxation which could be tapped if the government showed any serious political will to develop a more fair and equitable social welfare system. Many economists are agreed that there is potential for greatly increasing taxes on the wealthy which have been steadily declining as a percentage of the government's overall tax income for over a decade. For example, by EEC standards Ireland's corporation tax of between 0% and 10% is extremely low, compared to levels like 56% in West Germany and 45% in Britain. Indeed the next lowest to Ireland is Italy with corporation tax of 36%. Yet, as we have seen, the huge profits made by multinational companies here are largely repatriated to their country of origin thus offering little benefit to this country. The argument for higher taxes on these profits is overwhelming.

The ideas presented in this chapter are by no means radical. There are many other approaches to industrial and agricultural development, to coping with our debt crisis and to protecting the weaker sectors of society which could be put forward. It is difficult to generate debate, however, until such time as people feel a sense of urgency about the need to fashion alternatives. Nothing could be worse than the present impasse. If Ireland is to have any future, there is an urgent need to mobilise energies, begin a lively and far-reaching debate, to create hope that a better future is possible.

CHAPTER 9

Has Ireland a Future?: Building an Alternative

In the early hours of the morning of 18 June 1986, prisoners of the extremist neo-Maoist guerrilla group, *Sendero Luminoso* or Shining Path, began a co-ordinated uprising in three high-security prisons in Lima. Coinciding with a congress of the Socialist International then being held in the Peruvian capital, the uprisings were calculated to embarrass the government of President Alan Garcia and wrest an official guarantee to rescind plans to relocate the prisoners. Refusing to dialogue with the mutineers, the President instead ordered the security forces to put down the revolt. The result was frontal attacks on the three prisons using artillery, mortars, and rockets to subdue the prisoners. Some 250 prisoners are estimated to have perished in the attacks.

The final death count will never be known since the authorities refused to inform relatives of the deaths and ordered that victims be buried in common graves under cover of darkness. Subsequent investigations by Amnesty International concluded that at least 100 of the 124 prisoners killed in the attack on Lurigancho prison were killed in cold blood having surrendered to the security forces. No prisoner survived that attack. Of the 154 inmates on the island prison of El Fronton off Lima, only some 35 survivors were accounted for. According to Amnesty, however, the building was deliberately destroyed after some 60 to 90 prisoners had surrendered. Another 30 to 60 people were taken away by the Peruvian navy and have never been heard of since.

The prison massacres, the subsequent government blackout on information about what had really happened and the rumours and counter-rumours that gripped Lima in the following days and weeks, stunned Peruvians. Despite being accustomed to high-levels of official violence, the average Peruvian was profoundly shocked and disquieted. This was due firstly to the scale of the massacres and the government's attempts to exonerate itself from blame. But the events also provoked profound misgivings about the future of Peruvian society. The unstated question on everyone's mind was: 'Is this society going to disintegrate?'

So seriously was the question taken, that a number of prominent Peruvians announced that they were leaving the country, abandoning what they saw as a fast-sinking ship. The leading liberation theologian, Fr Gustavo Gutierrez, appealed at a large meeting of foreign missionaries that they also not abandon the country because, as he put it, 'the poor cannot leave and our place is to be with them.'

'We Can't All Live on a Small Island'

It is very sobering to live through such events and to witness at first hand the sense of desperation that can grip a whole people. In Peru the effect was dramatic but it led also to many individuals and groups redoubling their efforts not to give in to the many negative forces that seemed to be overtaking them. As a result of it all, the struggle for survival, for a better future, seemed to be underlined all the more.

At moments, the contemporary Irish situation gives rise to a similarly sobering assessment. The question may be less consciously formulated than it was in those grim days in Peru, but it is there nonetheless in the minds of many: Does Ireland have a future? While a sense of desperation and powerlessness comes palpably to the fore at moments like the Enniskillen massacre, such a sense lies heavily in the background of Irish life today. Those who work with young people, with the unemployed, with emigrants refer again and again to the widespread sense these groups have that Ireland has nothing to offer them. Those who can leave Ireland, do so with a sense of relief.

This was borne out by the dramatic results of a survey of

young people in the 16 to 24 age group carried out in August 1987. Asked the question 'Does Ireland offer young people a good future?' a massive 70% replied 'No'. Among the unemployed this climbed to 87% while among the employed it was still as high as 58%. Of the 25% who felt that Ireland does offer them a good future, a mere 5% were definite about their optimism. More than three-quarters of the 16 and 17 year-olds saw no future for themselves here while 62% of the 21 to 24 age group held that view. Not surprisingly in the light of these results, 60% said they had contemplated emigrating while 65% said they had no confidence in the country's political leaders to solve its economic problems.[1]

These results are indeed disturbing, if not surprising given the economic and social state of the country. But what is even more profoundly disturbing is the lack of any sense of urgency about them. Instead our political and business leaders blandly assert that we are getting the nation's finances in order, that inflation is at its lowest for many years and that we are experiencing a healthy trading surplus. Things are looking up, the future is bright, they claim.

The young, the unemployed and the poor cannot be blamed if they fail to share this optimism. While they may not be able to analyse it with any sophistication, they have experienced enough of Irish society to know what little hope it holds for them. What our political and business leaders fail to acknowledge is that none of the indices to which they point in themselves hold any hope for a large increase in employment or for any real economic growth or social change of the kind we urgently need. They appear concerned only about the impact of policies on the rich.

Instead the attitude of the government is far more accurately revealed by Mr Brian Lenihan's statement to *Newsweek* magazine that we should be proud of our emigrants. 'We regard them as part of a global generation of Irish people. We shouldn't be defeatist or pessimistic about it. We should be proud of it. After all, we can't all live on a small island,' he said.[2] At least Mr Lenihan has the advantage of honesty. He reveals what should be obvious from an examination of government policy – that they believe no substantial increase in employment on this island is possible and that the only hope for ambitious young people is to get out. Underlying such an attitude is the undeclared vision of Ireland as a dormitory society at the edge of the EEC, offering somewhere to raise the young, to care for the old, to keep the marginalised out of sight and to provide an enjoyable holiday location for the Community's workforce.

Much of this, of course, remains undeclared. Any suggestion that they might hold such a view would elicit a shocked reaction from our political or economic leaders; some of their staunch denials might even be sincere to the extent that they themselves do not see that this is the type of society they are building. But if they do not, it is because they fail to examine the growing trends which indicate that this is so. Some of these have been examined and pointed up in this book. They point in the direction of an ever richer elite presiding over a society in which large numbers are ever more marginalised and alienated. They point in the direction of growing police powers to control these marginalised groups. They point in the direction of under-funded health, education and social services ever more inadequate for the problems with which they have to cope. They point in the direction of a depopulated and ever more polluted countryside. The list could go on but the trends are clearly there for all to see.

Ireland today is in crisis. It is faced with fundamental choices about the type of future we want to build. The choices being made at the moment have been outlined in this book. They are not very difficult to see if we examine the evidence. Yet, they are being made quietly by our politicians and business leaders without their implications being explained, much less debated openly.

Indeed, as was shown all too clearly by the 'debate' on the Single European Act in 1987, our leaders seek to avoid anything more than cursory examination of the choices they are making, any questioning of where they will lead us. With typical arrogance they try to keep as much information as possible from the public or to mislead them through providing selective information. Instead they seem to expect an almost blind faith in the decisions they make on our behalf.

The issue of the single unified market to be achieved within the EEC by 1992 illustrates this. Having tried to keep the matter out of the public eye when the Single European Act was being formulated and agreed, our leaders are now lamenting the lack of awareness among the general public of its implications. As a result they now plan a campaign to educate the public about it!

Democracy depends on an informed and alert public. Controlling or even distorting the information we receive on important national issues augurs badly for the state of our democratic system. Similarly the existence of Section 31 and the ever more determined attempt to prevent certain Republican viewpoints being aired over our airwaves is a grave cause for concern. Politicians who prevent one type of views being publicly aired can easily decide that other sets of views are similarly unsuitable for the public to hear.

The problem in Ireland is that we are not being encouraged to debate our future; in fact we are being actively discouraged. Even in the midst of 20% admitted unemployment – a figure that could almost be doubled if those who have emigrated, those on 'schemes' and those who haven't signed on at all are added – no public debate takes place on what policies are needed to generate employment. Gone from our political vocabulary is the aspiration to 'full employment'. Few even bother to ask what has replaced it.

It is little wonder then that those who can, think of emigrating. It is little wonder that cynicism is widespread, that many take the prevailing sense of desperation and hopelessness for granted, as if there were no alternative. To this extent we are in a worse situation than the Peruvians referred to at the beginning of this chapter. At least they clearly saw the choices facing them: the slide into violent disintegration or the effort to strengthen the people's movement and the alternative culture and social organisation it was building from the grass-roots. In that situation there was an alternative available for which one could opt, there was a real choice.

Building an Alternative

Ireland urgently needs a real choice, an alternative around which those who presently see no hope for the future could gather. As was shown in Chapter Eight, alternative economic and social policies for a different future are available. But what needs to be addressed is the political paralysis which prevents us making such an option. How to break out of such a paralysis and build a different future is the principal lesson we can learn from the Latin American experience.

As the previous chapters have shown, such an alternative has been developed in a rich and diverse variety of ways throughout the region. It has grown as a response to the social and economic crisis facing the majority of Latin Americans. The more present-day capitalist society disintegrates, unable to satisfy even the most basic needs of the majority and resorting instead to severe repression in order to survive, the more has a grass-roots alternative been strengthened. Faced with the choice being made by the elites to perpetuate a status quo which increasingly marginalises them, the poor have made their choice to build a different kind of society. It is the only choice that can offer them hope for the future.

Making such a choice for building an alternative, however, has necessitated a psychological breakthrough. For long manipulated by politicians with their populist promises, the poor have had to cut the umbilical cord that perpetuated their dependence on the powerful. Learning about the structural nature of society has enabled them to understand that they are victims of a particular way of structuring society and that radical structural change is necessary if they are to have a share in society's wealth and power. As a result, they gain a sense of their own power and realise that such change is possible only through their own efforts. A healthy dose of scepticism replaces the former deference to authorities. Grass-roots and local initiatives replace the former dependence on the powerful, whether the state or private enterprise.

A similar psychological breakthrough needs to be made in Ireland. While many grass-roots initiatives have developed in response to the unemployment crisis of the 1980s, large numbers of those most directly affected by the crisis lack any sense of their own power. Instead of a constructive anger through which they might organise to challenge the policies and structures that marginalise them, most of the unemployed internalise a sense of shame and even guilt about their lot. This keeps them divided and competing with one another for the few jobs available. Few understand that they are victims of particular choices made by Ireland's political and business elite and even fewer believe that any alternative is possible.

Despite a marked lack of confidence in political leaders, as shown for example by the survey of young people outlined above, most Irish remain extremely dependent on them. This reveals a certain schizophrenia as widespread alienation from the major institutions of our society is combined with a continuing dependence on them. Much effort is spent trying to influence the authorities to the neglect of building awareness and solidarity among the marginalised.

No real alternative can grow until the victims of our society learn to see themselves as victims, until, as Paulo Freire put it to me, they can read their own reality. As outlined in Chapter Four, this will demand on-going programmes of conscientisation with particular emphasis on social analysis. For many in Ireland, and not just the poor, a kind of mystique seems to surround our economic problems whereby they are put beyond the pale of rational examination. As a result, they take on an almost divine inevitability leading to the widespread belief that no alternative is possible. This mystique must be urgently dissipated and clear analysis of economic issues be encouraged, particularly by those most victimised by present policies.

This highlights another problem inhibiting the growth of an alternative to the present malaise in Irish life. Most of the analysis being done on our contemporary situation starts out from a fundamentally conservative position. Our universities, from where one should expect a broad range of critical analyses to be emerging, by and large accept the narrow consensus which dominates our economic and social thinking. Unlike Latin America, there are no think-tanks in Ireland seeking to analyse society from the perspective of the poor and marginalised and provide well-researched alternatives to present policies. Those few thinkers who do work from such a perspective are easily marginalised as lone voices. Furthermore, the widespread indignation with which our politicians greeted Raymond Crotty's critique of and challenge to the Single European Act in 1987, indicates an unwillingness to acknowledge that more critical perspectives are even legitimate.

The absence of a more critical analysis of our problems, such as is widely available in a sophisticated form throughout Latin America, greatly impoverishes the policies and strategies of our political parties, particularly the left. It leaves those working on social analysis with grass-roots groups lacking a lot of the necessary groundwork to put flesh on the bones of their analysis. Finally, its absence allows the narrow consensus of our current orthodoxy to go unchallenged. It reinforces the sense of hopelessness and lack of choice about our future.

What characterises so much political and economic analysis in Ireland is that it is done from an elitist standpoint. Though some of it at least purports to speak on behalf of the poor, it does not arise out of their experience. Because it is not rooted in their world, it does not interpret their experience nor does it encourage them to work for change. The fundamental criterion for any worthwhile analysis of society must be that the oppressed can immediately identify with it, can say: 'Yes, that explains what happens to me and my neighbours.' That is the test of any authentic social analysis.

It is for this reason that much emphasis is put in this book on working to develop the awareness of the poor and marginalised and encouraging them to mobilise for change. It is they, more than any other sector of society, who should immediately understand the underlying trends in Irish life today because it is they who most suffer from them. Furthermore, since they have everything to gain by working to change the present system, they should be the most wholehearted in wanting to build an alternative. This obviously does not mean that other sectors should not similarly be conscientised and mobilised to work for a new society. But, as is so quickly verified by anyone involved in the work of conscientisation in Ireland today, it is the poor and marginalised who immediately understand and can relate to what is being revealed. Many other groups resist a view of society that starts with the experience of the marginalised and powerless.

This priority on the poor and marginalised supersedes to some extent the traditional priority put on the working class as an agent for radical social change. In an era of mass unemployment, some sectors of the working class have become a privileged class whose main interest is in protecting their jobs. On the other hand, many sectors of the working class, particularly women, are in low-paid and vulnerable jobs. To this extent they can be said to be among the marginalised of our society.

Building a People's Movement

If the only real hope for a better future for Ireland lies in developing an alternative, where do we look to see this happening today? One indication of just how extensive is the 'alternative movement' is gained from the thousands of entries in the *Alternative Ireland Directory*, listing everything from alternative energy groups to youth groups.[3] The political significance and potential of such a network is rarely adverted to, however. Within the wide range of groups that do exist, a number of sectors can be identified in which this potential is immediately obvious.

In response to the challenges of unemployment and growing poverty over recent years, a strong network of groups has developed. This includes centres for the unemployed, local co-operatives and job centres, education and community work groups, and many other locally-based initiatives. Many of these have a strong emphasis on conscientising and empowering the marginalised in our society. They are the closest we have got in Ireland to the *movimiento popular* in Latin America.

The growth of a more serious political left in Ireland complements this work at grass-roots level. The election of Tony Gregory was a direct result of this work and his role as a national political figure shows its potential. The presence of the Workers Party in the Dáil since the early 1980s, together with Jim Kemmy's Democratic Socialist Party, provide, for the first time, a more coherent vision of a socialist alternative. The new strength of the left within the Labour Party also offers hope that that party may give its backing to the developing socialist consensus on our major economic and social issues.

But appeal must be made to wider alternative movements in Irish life if a strong People's Movement is to be built which can embody and offer a real choice for the future. While these are primarily middle class movements, they have served to politicise sectors of this class and have on occasions shown their potential for wider popular appeal. Among these are the women's movement, Third World development and peace groups, the growing ecological movement and many cultural groups.

As was stated in Chapter Three, these embody much of the creativity present in Irish life today. They are, broadly speaking, sympathetic to one another and can on occasions like the referenda of recent years find common cause together. But, apart from such occasions, they remain fragmented, often content to be insignificant sub-cultures lobbying on issues that concern them. Their impact is therefore very limited. The surprise and bitter disappointment of their members at the results of those referenda, indicated to many of them just how unrepresentative of the wider society they are. But these results also showed the need for more systematic and on-going action if the alternative values and vision they espouse are ever to gain wider acceptance in Irish society.

A final movement that cannot be overlooked if any real People's Movement is to be built is the Republican movement. While it is tempting to overlook it since even mentioning it tends to cause profound divisions, it reminds us that the bitterly conflictive 'national question' cannot be left aside in any consideration of Ireland's future. The bitter differences of opinion that exist among progressive groups on the issue greatly weaken any challenge of the dominant conservative consensus.

As long as the Republican movement remains committed to armed struggle, there appears no hope that most alternative groups would ever consider an alliance with it. But if, under Gerry Adams' leadership, it opted to end the armed struggle or to use violence only in purely defensive circumstances, and concentrated instead on political work, that would dramatically change the conditions for its acceptance. Any move in that direction is to be actively encouraged.

What is missing so that these groups could make a greater impact on Irish life is a common agenda, a deeper analysis of our present malaise and a common vision of the future. While sectors of the women's movement or the ecological movement may have many difficulties with the left, for example, they allow these differences to blind them to the many basic aspirations they hold in common. Instead of functioning simply as lobby groups, seeking to influence policy on a specific range of issues, their impact could be all the greater if they saw themselves as being part of a People's Movement working together for more fundamental structural and cultural change in Irish society.

Alliances need to be built between different groups through which a common social vision could begin to take shape. This would have to be broad enough to articulate the different critiques currently challenging the dominant structures and values of Irish society, whether they be political, socio-economic, cultural or feminist. Out of the fragmented subcultures of the present, a new counter-culture must emerge, offering a coherent alternative project and bringing together a People's Movement to implement this project. This will entail a lot of change by many groups, not least the fragmented left.

Different left-wing groups will need not just to overcome the many bitter legacies of past divisions but also to respond more coherently and effectively to the needs of the marginalised. Many need to grow out of their traditional inclination to take control of groups and instead learn to enter into genuine alliances. Such fundamental critiques to traditional socialism as come from the feminist and the ecological movements will have to be grappled with in a serious and self-critical way. Traditional suspicions about christian groups will have to be overcome and their contribution appreciated. On the other hand, many groups committed to radical social change have a lot to learn from the left's critique of capitalism.

Obviously such a process of building alliances and discovering a common vision will not be easy. Some groups will seek to control it, afraid to trust 'the people' whom they so often rhetorically purport to represent. It can only happen on the basis of a shared concern to confront the reality of Irish life today, to uncover what is happening and to work together to change it. Unfortunately far too many groups who claim such concern seem more interested in propagating themselves and their prescriptions for change than in seeking to build an alternative of which they would simply be one small element.

More fundamentally, such a process would force a concentrated focus on the Irish reality itself rather than on ideological starting points whether they be socialist, christian, feminist or combinations of these. As was mentioned in Chapter Six, a similar breakthrough in Peru has helped the

left to overcome its profound ideological divisions and instead
find a common starting point.

Such a focus on the Irish reality is urgently needed. One
thing it would serve to overcome is the sterile reduction of
so many issues into a confrontation between secularising
liberals and clericalist traditionalists. While both groups are
strongly present on the Irish stage, a third option needs to
be presented, a popular socialist option. It might find fellow
cause with the secularising liberals on particular issues but it
needs to establish its own priorities, to many of which the
liberals would be staunchly opposed. There are many who
reject both the liberal and the traditionalist option: they want
a different choice for the future.

Conclusion

Many in Ireland are deeply concerned about what the future
holds. Even if there was never any real prospect of building
a society that would 'cherish all the children of the nation
equally,' at least certain attempts were made in the past which
seemed at the time to offer the hope of a better future for all.
De Valera's nationalist project from the 1930s to the 1950s
was one such attempt to build a strong economy under native
control. The multinational experiment of Lemass was a second
effort to boost economic and social development. Both have
proved failures, leaving a legacy of stagnation and despair. It
is obvious that a radical new direction is needed.

As has been stated on a number of occasions throughout
this book, however, what is most disturbing about our present
impasse is the sense of apathy and lack of urgency that
prevails. This alerts us to the fact that our problems cannot
be reduced simply to the economic and social. There is a
deeper cultural problem, a lack of will to confront and deal
with them. The future looks bleak indeed if present trends
are to be allowed prevail.

It is for this reason that the choice outlined in this book
appears a stark one. It is based not just on an analysis of the
contemporary situation in Ireland, but also on the many

similarities between Ireland and Latin America. These similarities stem from the fact that both are relatively under-developed economies suffering under the impact of today's more aggressive multinational capitalism. If this has posed a stark choice for many in Latin America, I see no reason why a similar stark choice does not face us here in Ireland. The choice is nothing less than working to define and build a popular socialist alternative.

Many might argue that the judgement is too sweeping, that we should give present policies a chance to prove themselves before deciding that such a radical re-orientation is required. But that poses the question – How long do we have to wait before we declare them a failure? Growing poverty and violence, declining employment, heavy indebtedness are all problems faced both by Ireland and by every Latin American capitalist country. Most of those countries have tried the austerity policies currently being implemented here and they had disastrous results for the majority of the population. When are we going to cry halt?

Focusing on the stark choice facing us, also encourages people to put their energies into building the alternative so urgently needed. This will involve not just a fundamental shift in economic and social policies and priorities but also in our values and ways of thinking as a society. In many places throughout this book, such a fundamental shift and what it might entail has been outlined.

A fundamental shift of this kind is usually called a revolution. I believe such is urgently needed in our social values as in our social structures. In countries like Nicaragua and Cuba, I have been able to witness just what a profound transformation such a 'fundamental shift' can cause, a transformation of social and personal relationships themselves. It can release energies and creativity, pent up and misdirected in our present society. While we have to discover our own indigenous way to bring about such a transformation, it is the only option that offers us a real hope and a better future for all.

Notes

Chapter 1

1. Stanislaus Kennedy, ed., *One Million Poor*, Turoe Press, Dublin, 1981.
2. John D Roche, *Poverty and Income Maintenance Policies in Ireland 1973-80*, Institute of Public Administration, Dublin, 1984, p. 160.
3. *Ibid.*, p. 135.
4. *Ibid.*, p. 239.
5. Statement from the AGM of the National Conference of Priests of Ireland, published in 'Unemployment: Challenge to Christians', A Doctrine and Life Special, Dominican Publications, Dublin, 1983, p. 65.
6. Roche, *op. cit.*, p. 5.
7. EEC Commission 1980 a, 'The Community and its Regions', European Documentation 1/80. p. 8.
8. Leslie Hamilton and Wolf-Dieter Just, *The Evolution of Regional Disparities in the European Community: An Ethical Perspective*, ERE, Rotterdam, 1981, pp. 31, 32.
9. Unpublished interview with author.
10. Hamilton and Just, *op. cit.*, p. 3.

Chapter 2

1. *The Irish Times*, 13 November 1987.
2. *The Irish Times*, 16 November 1987.
3. Helder Camara, *Spiral of Violence*, Sheed and Ward, London, 1971, pp. 25 and 30.
4. *Ibid.*, p. 34.
5. *Ibid.*, p. 34.
6. Oscar Romero, Fourth Pastoral Letter *The Church, Political Organisations and Violence*, English trans. CIIR, London, 1980. Extracts taken from section on violence, pars 69-77.
7. Pope Paul VI, Encyclical Letter: *Populorum Progressio*, par 31.
8. Romero, *op. cit.*
9. Quoted in *The Irish Times*, 30 October 1987.
10. Romero, *op. cit.*
11. Tim Pat Coogan, *Disillusioned Decades: Ireland 1966-87*, Gill and Macmillan, Dublin, 1987, p. 217.
12. Robert G. Crawford, *Loyal to King Billy*, Gill and Macmillan, Dublin, 1987, p. 118.
13. *Ibid*, p. 117.

Chapter 3

1. Ivor Browne, 'Mental Health and Modern Living', unpublished paper, June 1979.
2. *The Irish Times*, 8 July 1985.
3. Dolores Dooley, 'Expanding an Island Ethic', in *Ireland: Towards a Sense of Place*, Cork University Press, Cork, 1985, p. 48.
4. *Ibid.*, p. 49.
5. *Ibid.*, p. 53.
6. *Ibid.*, p. 57.
7. *Ibid.*, p. 57.
8. *The Tablet,* 20 June 1987.
9. Anthony Clare, in *The Crane Bag*, Vol. 7, No. 2, p. 175.

Chapter 4

1. Michael Fogarty, *'Irish Values and Attitudes'*, *The Irish Report of the European Values Study*, Dominican Publications, Dublin, 1984.
2. Michael Fogarty, *Irish Values*, Paper read at workshop, 14 January 1985, p. 18.
3. Paulo Freire, *Cultural Action for Freedom*, Penguin Books, Harmondsworth, 1972.
4. Published in *The Irish Times*, 21 January 1981.
5. Donal Dorr, *Spirituality and Justice*, Gill and Macmillan, Dublin, 1984, p. 189.
6. Seán J. Healy SMA and Brigid Reynolds SM, *Social Analysis in the Light of the Gospel*, Justice Office, CMRS, Dublin, 1983, and *Ireland Today,* Justice Office, CMRS, Dublin, 1985.
7. John Sweeney SJ, *Unemployment: Crisis or Opportunity*, Centre for Faith and Justice, Dublin, revised edition, 1987.

Chapter 5

1. 'Many Voices, One World: Report by the International Commission for the Study of Communications Problems' (MacBride Report), UNESCO, Paris, abridged edition, 1984, p. 191.
2. *Noticias Aliadas*, 20 January 1983.
3. Johan Galtung, 'Social Communication and Global Problems', in *Communication for All: New World Information and Communication Order*, Orbis Books, Maryknoll, 1986, p. 4 and 5.
4. Cf. Clarencio Neotti, *A Nova Ordem Mundial da Informacão e da Comunicacão*, Vozes, Petropolis, 1986, p. 28.
5. MacBridge Report, *op. cit.*, p. 218.
6. Conor Brady, 'Ownership and Control of the National Newspapers in Ireland', in *Is the Irish Press Independent?*, Media Association of Ireland. p. 6.
7. John Horgan, 'The Provincial Papers of Ireland', in *op. cit.*, Media

Association of Ireland, p. 12.

8. John Horgan, 'State Policy and the Press', in *The Crane Bag*, Vol. 8, No. 2, p. 51.

9. Michael D. Higgins, 'The Tyranny of Images', in *The Crane Bag*, Vol. 8, No. 2. p. 140.

Chapter 6

1. Gustavo Gutierrez, *The Power of the Poor in History*, SCM Press, London, 1983, p. 81.

2. Tom Garvin, 'Change and the Political System', in *Unequal Achievement: The Irish Experience 1957-1982*, Institute of Public Administration, Dublin, 1982, p. 38.

Chapter 7

1. Eduardo Galeano, in *Noticias Aliadas*, 19 February 1987.

2. Eduardo Galeano, in *Barricada*, English edition, 11 December 1986, p. 7.

3. *Ibid.*, p. 9.

4. *Ibid.*, p. 7.

5. Interview with author.

6. English translation of quotes from Mairtín Ó Cadhain 'Gluaiseacht na Gaeilge, Gluaiseacht ar Strae': 'Irish is the repossession of Ireland and the repossession of Ireland will save the Irish language.' 'Gluaiseacht na Gaeilge, Gluaiseacht ar Strae' is re-published in Bosco Costigan, *De Ghlaschloich an Oileáin*, Cló Iar-Chonnachta, Conamara, 1987, pp. 317-331.

7. 'It isn't only that Irish speakers should be involved in this struggle for the repossession of Ireland – it is the only thing that is worth while being involved in in Ireland – but it is our duty to lead and guide it. Let the Irish language be leading the revolution, and in this way let Irish be among the most progressive ideas in Ireland.'

8. '. . . to give back to the people of Ireland the possession of Ireland and all its wealth.'

9. 'It is the duty of Irish speakers to be socialists.'

10. '. . . Marx, Engels and Lenin would find proof there how true it is that the ruling class and the wealthy, the capitalists, are the first to abandon the learning and culture of the| people.'

11. Liam Mac Mathúna, *Pobal na Gaeilge*, Coiscéim, Dublin, 1987.

12. Eduardo Galeano, *Noticias Aliadas*, 19 February 1987.

Chapter 8

1. Cf. Eoin O'Malley, 'Creating Jobs in Irish Industry: The Example of the Engineering Sector', in *Studies*, Autumn 1987, pp. 263-272.

2. *Comment*, No. 3, February 1988, The Jesuit Centre for Faith and

Justice, p. 1.
3. *Ibid.*, p. 1.
4. O'Malley, *op. cit.*, p. 272.
5. Richard Cottrell, *The Sacred Cow*, Grafton Books, London, 1987, p. 34.

Chapter 9

1. *Irish Independent,* 4 December 1987.
2. Quoted in *The Irish Times,* 13 October 1987.
3. *Alternative Ireland Directory*, AID, Cork, 1987.

SIX GENERATIONS: LIFE AND WORK IN IRELAND FROM 1790
L.M. Cullen

Six generations represent only a short moment in the long history of human civilisation, but these six generations have brought more change in the way of life of the ordinary man and woman than came in the thousands of years before. From earliest times to the days of O'Connell, the speed of travel was no faster than that of a galloping horse; news of great events could take days even weeks to reach from one end of the country to another. This book describes the significant changes in everyday life — food, entertainment, household goods, working conditions, medicine, roads and communication — and what brought them about.

Louis Cullen, who is a lecturer in history in Trinity College, Dublin, based the material on original and pioneering research he has carried out over a number of years. The illustrations are drawn from a variety of sources including the National Gallery, the National Library, the London Illustrated News and from many locations all over Ireland.

For the older generations this book will recall a way of life in the countryside which has virtually disappeared and for the younger generation it will illuminate what life was like while historic events such as the '98 rising, O'Connell's repeal movement, the Fenians and 1916 were being enacted. For both parents and pupils, this book will serve as a useful companion to the Telefis Scoile series of the same title.

NORTHERN IRELAND:
WHO IS TO BLAME?
Andrew Boyd

Why did Westminster remain silent while the unionists operated a permanent machine of dictatorship under the shadow of the British Constitution?

Why have the Southern governments let Britain hand over the lives and liberties of the minority to the Orange Institution?

Is the weakness of Labour in the north due to the fact that neither the NILP nor the ICTU have ever had any policies that would distinguish them from the unionists?

What help have Fianna Fáil, Fine Gael and the Labour Party offered to the minority north of the border?

Northern Ireland: Who is to Blame? examines the events and political attitudes and ideologies in both islands that have brought Northern Ireland to its present state of dangerous instability.

THE CROZIER AND THE DÁIL: CHURCH AND STATE 1922-1986
John Cooney

The remark that Stormont was 'a Protestant parliament for a Protestant people' has frequently been countered with the accusation that the Republic is a Catholic State for a Catholic people. Is the Irish State unduly influenced by the Church of the majority? This question came painfully and divisively to the fore in the 1980s with the abortion referendum and with the liberalisation of the laws on contraception. The question of who rules the country — the crozier or the Dáil — lay at the centre of the divorce referendum.

In *The Crozier and the Dáil* John Cooney examines Church-State relations since the foundation of the state.

IS IRISH CATHOLICISM DYING?
Peadar Kirby

— Has the Catholic Church any major contribution to make to the task of building a new society of justice and peace in Ireland?

— Is there a growing inability on the part of the Church to influence public opinion?

— Are church leaders out of touch with the real needs of the people?

— As a wealthy property owner, does the Church sometimes find itself sharing the same outlook and values as the rich?

— Does the Church feel threatened by civil rights movements?

— Why has the Church played such a major role in developing a public awareness of the political and economic injustices in Central America, Philippines, etc. and not tackled injustice and the gross inequalities at home with the same vigour?

— Should the Church be helping to make rebels of the poor by helping them to stand up to their oppressors?

— Is Northern Ireland, with its continuing violence and deep-seated religious division, a symbol of the final failure of our conventional church allegiances and their halting Christianity?

SOUL OF FIRE
A Biography of Mary MacSwiney
Charlotte H. Fallon

Born during the Home Rule for Ireland Campaign, Mary MacSwiney was aware of the political situation in Ireland from an early age, though hers was not a politically involved home. Her awareness of Ireland's fight for self-government was sharpened during the Irish cultural revival of the early 1900s, her education and associations, and the political activities of her brother Terence.

At this time, however, Mary's energies were directed toward gaining voting rights for women, an issue she saw plainly as a matter of justice. With the rise of the Sinn Fein movement after 1912, her interest gradually shifted away from woman suffrage to nationalist concerns. With the Rising of 1916 and the declaration of the Republic, Mary came to believe that Ireland's desire for freedom, peace and prosperity could be best served by an Irish Republic totally outside the sceptre of British rule. From 1916 on, her life was devoted to the Republic and efforts at making it a functioning reality for all Irish men and women.

Her political career as a doctrinaire Republican brought her into conflict with the Catholic Church, the Free State Government against whom she waged two lengthy hunger strikes, those moderates within Ireland who believed in the 'stepping stone' approach to independence, and Eamon de Valera who she believed had forsaken the principles of 1916.

Her life provides information about women's issues in Ireland, Irish-American relations as she made two extensive fund raising tours of the United States, Irish Nationalism, the splintering of the Republican Movement, the rise of Irish Republican militancy, and the pervasive role of the Catholic Church in politics as well as in the rest of society.

THE PURSUIT OF MEANING
Joseph Fabry

The Pursuit of Meaning is written for the millions of people who are healthy but believe they are sick, because they feel empty; for those who are looking for meaning in frantic activity, in money, power, speed, excitement, sex, alcohol, and drugs, or in the pursuit of happiness for happiness' sake; for those who are looking for meaning in laws and rules and dogmas rather than searching for it personally. Every mature person has been expelled from his own paradise and lived through his own concentration camp. To help man endure this has always been the tasks of prophets, priests, philosophers and educators. Now they are joined by psychologists. Logotherapy supplies one contemporary answer to man's age-old problem of how to live after the expulsion and how to find meaning during and after the trials of sufferings.

Dr Viktor Frankl is the leading figure in what has come to be called the Third Viennese School of Psychotherapy. His writings represent the most important contributions in the field of psychotherapy since the days of Freud, Adler and Jung. He is the author of nineteen books and his work has been translated into fourteen languages including Japanese and Chinese. His book *Man's Search for Meaning* has sold over a million copies and recently his work *The Doctor and the Soul* was published by Penguin books.

The Pursuit of Meaning is a guide to the theory and application of Viktor E. Frankl's logotherapy and is a very readable book which will appeal to anyone interested in the purpose of life. It is an excellently and clearly written, authoritative and comprehensive presentation of Frankl's system, probably more complete than can be found in any one volume by Frankl himself. It was first published in English in the USA and is now in its third edition. It has been translated and published in Italian, German, Spanish and Japanese.